MISSION COMPLETED

T. S. MOONEY
of Londonderry

1907—86

Issued by a group of Mr. Mooney's colleagues and published under T.S.M. Books from 4 Harmony Hill, Lisburn, Co, Antrim BT27 4EP, to which all orders and correspondence should be directed. Phone: 08462/81017.

Published by T.S.M. Books
4 Harmony Hill, Lisburn, Co. Antrim BT27 4EP

Printed by The Universities Press (Belfast) Limited.

MISSION COMPLETED

T. S. MOONEY
of Londonderry

1907—86

It is an extraordinarily great thing to have known such a man of whom we cannot recall one single misdemeanour of which we might feel ashamed, or one unworthy action for which we might have to apologise.

— JOHN T. CARSON

T.S.M. BOOKS

iii

"T.S."   Photo by T. S. McCarter

Foreword

By the Moderator of the General Assembly
(Rt. Rev. Dr. Robert Dickinson)

"The memory of the just is blessed" Prov. 10:7

When I became a student at Magee University College, Londonderry in 1944 I quickly discovered that there were certain associations by which one's theology was identified either as 'evangelical' or otherwise. 'Evangelicals' were to be found, amongst other places, at the Crusader Class which met on Sunday afternoons in the Presbyterian Working Men's Institute in the Diamond under the leadership of a gentleman called Mr. T. S. Mooney, of whom hitherto I had not heard. I was soon to discover, however, that to know this spiritual giant of a man and to share his godly influence, wisdom, counsel, encouragement and friendship was a rare and profound privilege.

In the intervening years it was a great joy to me to be closely associated with him in many evangelical enterprises both within our Presbyterian Church and in wider fields of Christian work and witness. Over the past 40 years and more there have been few aspects of the life and witness of our Church at home and overseas which have not benefited from and been influenced decisively by 'T. S.' either directly, or through those ministers and elders who themselves have been to a greater or lesser degree moulded by the impact of his life and work.

Magee has gone and with it much that was irreplaceable in the formation and fellowship of the ministry of our Church. 'T. S.' too has finished his course amongst us. For me to have been asked to contribute to this memoir is honour indeed. As I said on the occasion of his funeral service:

> "As one who shared and treasured his friendship for 42 years, both at the personal level and in many aspects of the life and witness of our Church, of which he was so distinguished a son

v

and servant, I should like to express the gratitude of all of us whose lives have been touched and influenced in the most sacred ways by the evangelical faith and fervour of one of Christ's rare and steadfast warriors.

His passing has brought to an end a unique era in the life of our own Church in particular, and in the cause of evangelical work and witness not only in Ireland but across the world. We shall miss him very sadly, but we shall ever be proud and grateful to have known and shared the triumphant faith, the transparent loyalty and the transcendent hope of T. S. Mooney, which are now eternally vindicated and perfectly fulfilled in the great assembly of 'the church of the first-born who are in heaven'. To God be the glory!"

We shall ever be grateful also to those who have prepared or contributed to this reminder of one whose courage, modesty and devotion to the cause of Christ and of His Gospel are already realised in that

> ". . . joy all joys beyond!
>   To see the Lamb who died,
> For ever there enthroned,
>   For ever glorified,
> To give to Him the praise
>   Of every triumph won,
> And sing, through endless days,
>   The great things He hath done."

The Manse, Tobermore,
Co. Londonderry.
April 1986

Contents

Frontispiece

The Contributors

Rev. Eric M. Borland, B.A. — senior minister of Burnside Presbyterian Church, Portstewart.

Very Rev. Dr. David Burke, B.A. — senior minister of Hamilton Road Church, Bangor.

Very Rev. Dr. John T. Carson, B.A. — senior minister of Trinity Church, Bangor.

Rev. Dr. Alan Flavelle, B.A., B.D. — minister of Lowe Memorial Church, Finaghy, Belfast.

Rev. S. L. Smiley Fullerton, B.A. — minister of Newcastle Presbyterian Church, Co. Down.

Rev. Malcolm McN. W. Hare, B.A., B.D. — minister of St. Kentigern's Church of Scotland, Kilmarnock.

Mr. James McDonald, M.B.E. — Former N.I. organising secretary of the Bible Society and honorary secretary of the Portstewart Convention.

Rev. Edgar S. McKinney, M.Th., B.D. — minister of Kilfennan Presbyterian Church, Londonderry.

Mr. R. John Magowan, B.A., D.A.S.E. — Senior Master in Foyle and Londonderry College and leader of the Crusader Class in that city.

Rev. James Philip, M.A. — minister of Holyrood Abbey Church of Scotland, Edinburgh.

The Editor's Acknowledgements

A book structured as this one is could never have become an accomplished fact without the generous help of many people. Thanks are therefore due all round:

* to a great team of contributors each of whom treated his part as a labour of love and kept strictly to a very tight time schedule; and who, in order to avoid the inevitable overlapping, showed their trust and confidence in allowing a certain amount of editorial 'blue-pencil' in preparing the final typescript.

* to the Rt. Rev. Dr. R. Dickinson (Moderator of the General Assembly) for his gracious Foreword and his encouragement all along.

* to the Rev. Edgar McKinney and his ever-helpful people in Kilfennan Presbyterian Church, who so spontaneously gave us access to congregational records and permission to use anything that was useful for our purpose. Also for the promise of much appreciated financial backing and support.

* to the following for permission to use their photographs viz. Rev. Wm. Leetch (cover, front), Mrs. M. McCloskey (cover, back), and Mr. T. S. McCarter (that on page vi). Also to Mr. Nevin Hall, Mr. Mooney's nephew (page 8) and Mr. Wm. Anderson, another kinsman (page 9), to Mr. T. Kydd for the line drawings of Gt. James Street and Kilfennan churches and to Miss Christine Boal for other artwork.

* to Mr. Alex, Rankin and Mr. Wm. McCloskey for the use of tributes paid to T.S. in the Londonderry C.W.U. Also to the Editor of *Evangelical Voice* for permission to use the article, *Zion's Courts* which appeared in that magazine in 1977 and to the Rev. Professor Robert McCollum for drawing our attention to it.

* to the Rev. Malcolm Hare for his painstaking work in abridging the original addresses of Mr. Mooney which now appear as Appendices II and IV. This is never an easy thing to do, not least when T.S. was the speaker.

* to Mr. John Magowan and his fellow Crusader leaders for their constant encouragement in the background; to Rev. Ivor F. Smith to whom more is owed than he is probably aware of; and especially to Mr. J. Hubert Martin without whom this book might simply never have got off the ground. Also to Mrs. Margaret Martin for her meticulous reading of proofs.

GREATHEART
How he discovered his life's work

*Mr. Greatheart, you should know, was Interpreter's armed
servant and he dwelt at Interpreter's house. From here he
was called to guide, and teach, and defend pilgrims on
their way to the Celestial City. Greatheart was not long
back from his strenuous efforts with Mr. Fearing when a
new party of pilgrims arrived, a mother and her four boys,
and they needed a guide.*

*"The Interpreter," Bunyan says at this point, "called for a
man servant of his, one Greatheart and bid him take sword
and helmet and shield, and take these and conduct them to
the house called Beautiful, at which place they will rest
next. So he took his weapons and went before them, and
the Interpreter said, 'God Speed' ".*

CHAPTER ONE

The Early Years

In his book, "Radiant Certainty", Alistair Maclean gives this advice: "Read the big biographies . . . they are the geography of man's endeavour. They compel you to climb to the peak of another's achievement, where you will find the air bracing and the view purified." What we present here is not a "big" biography, but it will enable you to share something of the exhileration of one man's endeavour.

A Minister in the Making?

T.S. claimed to be "a Derry man", not only because he spent all his working life in the Maiden City, but because his earliest years were lived out in the quiet countryside a few miles to the west of the inter-county border. He was born on 6th February 1907, and his forebearers were to be found among the Covenanting and Original Secession congregations in the area. He himself was brought up in the Dromore Original Secession Church, where from childhood he sat under the spell of the Rev. Edward White. Mr. White was from Co. Cavan and served for a time as a missionary in India. He had not only taken the theological course at the O.S. College, but had also done some study under the highly-gifted and greatly-loved Professor A. B. Davidson at New College. When asked to describe Mr. White's ministry T.S. said: "he preached without paper; his material was always well-prepared; and he invariably 'homed-in' on Jesus Christ' ". Such a ministry was not without effect on the homes and hearts of the people. Margaret, T.S.'s only sister, can recall Sunday afternoons of 'play Church', when T.S. was always the preacher and she was the congregation.

T.S. confessed that even as a boy he liked to learn the Catechism, and often pointed out in later years that it appealed to him because it was precise in statement, logical in arrangement, and evangelical in doctrine. To a large extent his own preaching was to reflect that pattern.

1

The news reached T.3. in Derry that Mr. White was due to preach his final sermon in Dromore Church on a certain Sunday. A friend offered to drive him down for the morning service and T.S. was delighted at the opportunity of being present at a service which marked the end of forty years of ministry. It was a sermon he would never forget, based on Deuter. 8:2: "You shall remember all the way which the Lord your God has led you these forty years . . .". Mr. White spoke of (1) the mercies of the way, (2) the friends of the way, (3) the sins of the way. As he came to the conclusion, Mr. White said, "I give God thanks that the dear Saviour who redeemed me by His blood has been the sum and substance of every sermon I have preached from this pulpit." A magnificent achievement for any preacher — and an admirable aim for any aspiring preacher.

A New Beginning

For many years the numbers attending the National School at Cullyvenny had been declining. It became, first, a one-teacher school and eventually it was forced to close. The school-house had two distinct associations for T.S. Here he received the earliest elements of his education, and here he was brought to find new life in Christ. Soon after the closure of the school, his father, who had been Chairman of the Management Committee, was approached by a man who was held in high repute in the neighbourhood for permission to use the school-building for an inter-denominational mission. This was readily granted, and for a period of six weeks two Faith Mission pilgrims, Mr. Alex Fullerton and Mr. W. D. Collinge, conducted a series of services. Mr. Collinge had formerly been a Music Hall artiste and T.S., now on the verge of his teens, was fascinated by the attractive and forthright presentation of the gospel. He attended every night, eventually yielding to the claims of Christ and becoming "a new creature in Christ Jesus".

Immediately after the end of the mission a Prayer Union was formed. It met every Monday night and the emphasis was on fellowship, Bible-teaching and Prayer. It was in this setting that T.S. first opened his mouth in public to speak and to pray.

During his teen-age years he found a continual battle with doubt, doubt not only about his own salvation but even about the very existence of God. It was a long time before he could be satisfied that it was not what he felt, but what God said, that mattered. In later years he often quoted the lines:

"I'm safe because I'm sheltered by Jesus' precious blood,
And I'm sure because He promised and He cannot break His word."

He also used to quote with approval the words of the Shorter Catechism: "The benefits which in this life do accompany or flow from justification. adoption, and sanctification, are, assurance of God's love, peace of conscience, joy in the Holy Ghost, increase of grace, and preseverance therein to the end."

Schooldays in Coleraine

His school days were, in his own words, "uneventful". After leaving Cullyvenny, he attended the Irish Society (Elementary) School in Coleraine for a period of two years. He then moved on to the Coleraine Academical Institution where he was a student for nearly four years under the Headmastership of Mr. T. J. Beare. He claimed that the school made little mark on him, as he certainly left little mark on the school. His one abiding memory of life at Inst. was of a rather strange relationship which he had with his History master. The teacher was an avowed agnostic, so it was not surprising that T.S. and he often crossed swords in debate, sometimes taking up a whole period, to the delight of his fellow-pupils. Thus we can see that early on he was willing and able to take a stand as Mr. Valiant-for-the-Truth. It is interesting to note that it was with this master that he carried on a correspondence for a number of years after leaving school. T.S. was greatly saddened by the news that, because of his outspoken, anti-Christian opinions the teacher was dismissed from his post and eventually took his own life.

A short stay in Belfast

Because his father's sister was suffering from terminal cancer, the family found it necessary to move for a time to Belfast where they could give her the necessary attention. T.S. in fact only remained in Belfast from Easter 1924 till January 1925. It was, he said, a bonus during those months to be a member of Newington Congregation then enjoying the ministry of the Rev. T. M. Johnstone. Of him T.S. said, "He was always outspoken on the

3

right side!" I have often heard him describe with enthusiasm how Newington Church was packed from floor to ceiling for the evening service, a sight not often seen even in those days of pulpit giants and large congregations.

A Turning of the Ways

It was his life-long ambition to be a minister or, failing that, to be a lawyer. During the months in Belfast he studied at Shaftesbury House, better known locally simply as "Renshaw's", in preparation for a scholarship examination which could open the door to the ministry. Unfortunately, when he sat for the examination, under the auspices of the Irish Society, he came second on the pass list and thus missed the scholarship which would have secured his entrance to the university.

In his own words "The Bank was the last place I wanted to go". Was not a higher hand at work and was he not being designated to a different ministry?

His father suggested that he should submit an application for the Bank. He was nominated by Mr. John Hezlett, then manager of the Belfast Bank in Coleraine, and eventually he was appointed to the Derry office.

There are two aspects of his service with the Bank which are worthy of comment. It has often been alleged that the Bank created a special post to enable him to remain in Derry. In fact, this was not the case. There was a position in the office that they had found difficult to fill. T.S., on being approached, seemed both willing and able to cope with it. The Manager put him in charge for a somewhat indefinite period. Later on, when the Manager learned of his desire to remain in Derry, he saw to it that he would not be transferred. As he said, "I have had the privilege of forty-five years unbroken service in the one Branch, without ever handling cash." The other thing concerned the Portstewart Convention in which Mr. R. L. McKeown had sought to foster his interest. T.S. pointed out that with his commitments in the Bank, it was not possible for him to attend. Two of the Convention office-bearers, Mr. R. H. Stephen Richardson and Mr. Robert Clyde, were substantial customers of the Belfast Bank, and they wrote to the Head Office requesting that T.S. should be given leave-of-absence for four days each year to attend the

4

Convention. This request was granted, and for thirty years T.S. was very much part of the Convention scene.

Beginnings in Derry

It was a kindly Providence that gave him the privilege of staying with the three Pollock sisters who were second cousins of his father. Not only did they keep open house, but from the beginning they encouraged him to invite to 13 Rosemount Terrace anyone who was in need of fellowship or Christian counsel. On his first Saturday in Derry he had a call from a well-known businessman, Mr. Joseph Goligher, who was secretary of the Christian Workers' Union. During a short period when the family lived near Bushmills, T.S. and Mr. Goligher had become friends. "Uncle Joe", as he was known, often came down to Bushmills on a Sunday afternoon to help with an open-air service which was held at the Square and with an indoor evangelistic service held in the Hamill Hall of the Presbyterian Church. That Saturday he invited T.S. for lunch and to a house-meeting at which T.S. gave his testimony for the first time in Derry. This friendship quickly ripened and was to prove beneficial to many people through the C.W.U. work in the city.

Although he had gone with the Pollock sisters to the Convenanting Church on his first Sunday, on the following Sunday he worshipped in Great James Street, thus forging a link that was to become an essential part of his future life and work. He had been invited by George Hanna, nephew of the well-known Judge Hanna and this invitation was reinforced by a conversation which he had with Mr. Andrew Morrison, a Great James's Street elder. Soon afterwards he attended a celebration to mark the twenty-fifth anniversary of Dr. Thompson's installation in the congregation. Sometime later he was invited to propose the Adoption of the Reports at the Annual General Meeting, later being elected to serve on the Committee, and, later still, to be a member of Session. From the beginning of his membership the well-being of Great James Street seems to have been written deeply on his heart.

T.S. was immensely proud to be "a Derry man". He used to say that Derry had given three great things to the world: "(1) a great tune — 'The Londonderry Air'; (2) a great hymn — 'There is a green hill'; and (3) a great watch-word — 'No surrender' ". I used

5

to banter him by asking: no surrender to what? To the Roman Catholic Church? To its unbiblical teaching? Or could it be with some no surrender to a legitimate claim for social justice and civil rights? Or no surrender to any attempt to change the status quo? For a long time T.S. tended to brush aside such questions. He, like so many Ulster Protestants, was blinded by a comfortable pietism to the urgency of social issues. Certainly T.S. was singularly unaware of the social and political pressures that were building up as in a cauldron, pressures which at a later date would burst both upon City and Province. It must be said to his credit, however, that hard biblical thinking brought him, during the seventies, to recognise the need for radical change and for constructive dialogue with the Roman Catholic Church and its people.

College days

He soon established himself in Magee University College, if not as an undergraduate, then certainly as a friend and confidant of the student body. He quickly developed contacts with the students, especially those who belonged to the Evangelical Union. Sensing that this man had something worthwhile to say, and an unusual ability for saying it, they invited him to speak first at their informal meetings and then at their regular Monday meeting. He was able to expound the Scriptures and to apply their message in a way that was singularly relevant to students. As he grew in stature as an expositor of the Word, they invited him to give several series of Bible studies, from the notes of which some ministers still get inspiration for their sermons. But it was not only in public ministry but in personal contacts that T.S. helped many students. The door of 13 Rosemount Terrace and later 9 Clarence Avenue was always open; there was always an ample supply of home-baked goodies; and, especially at the week-ends, T.S. seemed to have unlimited time and patience to sort out problems. Like that of John Mark's mother in Jerusalem, this was a home in which people knelt to pray, from which people went on service and to which people came in need.

T.S.'s work among students was recognised in later years when, as a Presbyterian elder, he was invited to give the Bible Readings at the Swanwick General Conference of the Inter-Varsity Fellowship. At the welcome meeting he was surrounded by several dignitaries of the Anglican Church, some of whom had taken part at the beginning of the meeting. When T.S. stood before that crowded audience, he began: "What shall I say by way of introduction? 'Canons to the right of me, canons to the left of me, volleyed and thundered. With prayer in my heart I hope that a few random shots from a humble Ulster rifle will not be too far off target' "? This, of course, brought the house down. He gave three masterly expositions of two chapters from Isaiah. The Biblical content, the logical analysis, the stylistic flair, the apt allusions, all this made a distinct impression, though it has to be admitted that some of the English students found T.S.' brand of the Queen's English difficult to grasp. Not a few of them took delight in mimicking one whose speech and gesture were beyond their ken.

What were the secrets learned and applied in these early years? He loved God's word and rejoiced to unfold its treasures to others. He continued steadfastly in prayer, and his prayers were always aimed at a specific target. He was wide in his sympathies, welcoming fellowship with Christians from many denominations, yet never betraying his loyalty to the local church. He developed his gifts by self-discipline and training so that they might be of maximum usefulness in the service of his Lord. He was magnanimous towards those with whom he disagreed and never allowed theological controversy to embitter his relationships. In a word, he was Christ's man.

On several occasions during the late fifties he and I holidayed together. One day we were touring in the island of Skye when the cloud had settled on the fields and the surrounding hills were wreathed in a thick mist blown in from the sea. He was anxious to visit the birth-place of a distinguished Scottish Churchman in a townland called "The Braes". The site was not marked on any map so we found it difficult to locate. On a narrow road we met a shepherd herding his sheep. We had some conversation with him about the weather and then I asked him: "Can you tell us what is the best way to The Braes?" He took a long pause and then with a fascinating twinkle in his eye he said: "There is but one way." He gave us precise directions, and as we motored on T.S. said to me: "There is an illustration you will not soon forget". Indeed there is but one way — to forgiveness of sins, to the hope of heaven, to the joys of life at its best — and that way is Christ. This T.S. said in so many different ways, to so many different people, that many of us will never forget. This truth, grasped so clearly in these early years, was to bear rich fruit in the years that were yet to be.

Alan Flavelle

T.S. with the Misses Pollock (pp 5-6, 51-52).

The Church of Mr. Mooney's boyhood at Dromore, Co. Londonderry.

> *Above a house of weathered stone.*
> *A plain old house of God.*
> *The summer hum of honey bees,*
> *Our Sabbath peace unflawed,*
> *Our green God's acre in the trees,*
> *Our plain old house of God.*
>
> *Such things are tethers to my feet*
> *When my departure nears;*
> *These, and the old old friends I meet,*
> *Unmatched throughout the years,*
> *Who learned with me in days long gone*
> *That two and two make four,*
> *And toed with me a chalk line drawn*
> *Upon a schoolroom floor.*

From W. F. Marshall's poem "TULLYNEIL" in I'm Livin' in Drumlister.
(Used by kind permission of Margaret Marshall).

Cullyvenny old school.

9

GREATHEART
and what he meant to the four boys

Then said James, the youngest of the boys, "Pray, sir, be persuaded to go with us, and help us, because we are so weak and the way so dangerous as it is.

* * *

Christiana and Mercy were afraid but Matthew said, "Mother, fear nothing as long as Mr. Greatheart is to go with us and be our conductor."

* * *

Then they went forward and began to go up the hill, up to the Prince's Arbour. Then Greatheart took the little boy by the hand and led him up thereto.

CHAPTER TWO

The Crusader Leader

Crusaders was T. S. Mooney's first love, of that there is no doubt. How often was he heard to say "I wouldn't swop my Crusader Class for any pulpit in the General Assembly" or "I have never taken any engagement which took me away from the Class on a Sunday afternoon." His instruction for his tombstone confirms the place Crusaders had in his heart for, after giving the essential details of name, date etc. he simply requested ... for fifty years the leader of the Londonderry Crusader Class ... "with Christ which is far better".

Crusaders, today a nationwide union of Bible Classes for boys and girls of secondary school age, began in London in 1906. The first class in Ireland was formed some eight years later in Dublin, and the first class in Northern Ireland, Belfast Central, was formed in 1927 under the leadership of F. S. A. Andrews and Dick Paisley. The Rev. Dr. John Carson spoke at the Central Class on a number of occasions and, on coming to Magee College in October 1930, he, together with the Very Rev. Dr. James Dunlop, encouraged T.S. to start a class in the Maiden City. Their efforts were successful and, on Sunday, 2 November, 1930 the Londonderry Crusader Class met for the first time — 9 boys and 3 leaders, John Carson, Duncan Gordon and T. S. Mooney are recorded in the attendance book for that day. For T.S. this was the beginning of a life's work which continued for fifty years until he resigned as a leader in December 1980. Throughout that period of time he approached the task with characteristic singleness of purpose as he aimed to give each boy "a Book in his hand, a Saviour in his heart and a purpose in his life."

His contribution to Crusaders was immense. The Union camp at Castlerock grew out of a camp started by the Londonderry Class in 1932. T.S. was the Commandant of this camp from its inception until 1972. He held a similar position at the Easter House Party which was held at Stricklands in Bangor from 1948 until 1970. For many years he was chairman of the Northern Ireland Area Committee and his overall contribution to

Crusaders was recognised in 1978 when he was elected a Vice-President of the Union.

When successive generations of Crusaders think of T.S. many pictures emerge. Those of an early generation think of the dingy room at the top of the 14 rickety stairs in the Presbyterian Working men's Institute in the Diamond with its platform at one end — the fireplace on one side of it, the piano on the other and rows of Crusaders sitting on hard forms. It was here that every year was begun and ended with 'There is a green hill far away' and an emphasis laid on the vital truth that 'there was *no other* good enough to pay the price of sin, *He only* could unlock the gate of heaven and let us in.' It was here that the opening prayer was always said "standing to attention, heads erect" and it was here that Badges and Bibles were always presented while the hymn 'Ashamed to be a Christian' was sung. Later generations recall the more luxurious surroundings of the Royal Sailors' Rest in Foyle Street with its fine, oak-panelled walls, shiny pine floor and intricately woven cloth on the table on the platform, while recent generations think of the Devotional Room of Ebrington Presbyterian Church. Many recall the Birthday "Squashes" in the Lecture Hall of Gt. James Street Presbyterian Church when Ronnie "Mac" came across from Coleraine to take the games.

There were the hair raising drives to Camps, Houseparties and Sports with T.S., crouched so low behind the wheel, hat at a rakish angle, that his view of the road, if existent at all, could only have been through the steering wheel. How he used to knock the car out of gear and free wheel down the Glenshane Pass — and this a mere prelude to doing the "ton" on the Toome straight! Others think of him at camp striding around in that well worn bomber jacket which gave him a distinctly Churchillian air; the silver whistle with which he brought the raucous, hungry, sweaty campers to order before delivering one of his distinctive graces — "on us and these Thy blessing please" or "grant us, Lord, a Father's blessing with a Father's gifts." All fondly recall his marvellous inability to sing in tune the hymns he loved. "There is plenty of music in me but it all gets spoiled on the way out," he used to say regularily.

From a human point of view T.S. was a most unlikely Crusader leader. He had very few of the interests which one normally associates with boys. His sporting ability was non existent, nor had he any interest in sport. He had no interest whatever in pop music, modern fashions was not his scene and the electronic revolution passed him by. Why did he have such a profound influence on successive generations of Crusaders for more than half a century? Why did Crusaders flock from all arts and parts to pay tribute to him at the fortieth Anniversary Dinner of the Londonderry Class? Why did money flood in at the fiftieth Anniversary to send him on a holiday to the west coast of Canada — a trip which meant so much to him. Why was it that all these generations were represented at his graveside on that icy cold January afternoon — one will long remember one of the "original nine" who met in November 1930 standing side by side with two first year students who had returned from England especially for his funeral.

Surely the real secret of T.S.'s "success" as a Crusader leader was his prayer life. Being basically a shy man, he did not talk much about this but those who shared rooms with him at various Crusader functions recall how he was up each morning at 6.00 a.m. with his various prayer lists stretched out before him on his open Bible. He once advised a young Crusader leader to "pray for every one of the boys in your class with the roll book open in front of you". He certainly practised what he preached and only eternity will reveal how many hours he spent in prayer for the boys in his class. He maintained this prayerful interest in his boys right to the end of his life — amongst the papers in the Bible at his bedside was the press cutting of a photograph of a former Crusader who was no longer showing much interest in spiritual things.

His prayerful concern for his boys led him to take a real, practical interest in each one of them. He was always at Class at least half an hour before the starting time to give himself plenty of time to greet the boys on their arrival, to chat to them and find out more about them. For years, junior Crusaders were invited in small groups to have Sunday tea at No. 9 Clarence Avenue. That their leader should take such an interest in them made a profound impression on many young Crusaders. One said "from first going to Crusaders Mr. Mooney got to know my name and from then on he took a consistent interest in my life." Another states, "I will always remember T.S. as being someone who took a personal interest in me as an individual. If I ever missed

Crusaders for one reason or another, he would be at my door during the week to say, "missed you last Sunday' ". "After my father died, Mr. Mooney asked me about my mother every Sunday for a year as we filed out at the end of class" was the vivid recollection of another.

At Camp and House Party also, T.S. made it his business to get to know each boy and ensure that he had a good chat with him. While others were engaged in frenzied athletic activity, either on the beach at Castlerock or on the pitch at Stricklands Glen, T.S. would spend his time chatting to boys and encouraging them to enjoy camp. Here many friendships were cemented to last a life time.

Although he enjoyed the company of the juniors he really felt more at ease with the senior boys in the Class. It was his delight to have them in for an evening around the fire to hear how they were getting on and to discuss whatever problems they might have. Here he was in his element as he dealt with questions the boys put to him about different aspects of the faith. Here he would demonstrate his unique ability to stand back from a situation and sum matters up with marvellous spiritual common sense, like the evening a discussion on faith and healing was getting increasingly confused. T.S., who had been quiet to this point, was asked for his opinion and, with a faint smile, he simply said, "well, from my reading of the Bible it seems that some people were healed and some were not." Here, too, he would encourage his boys to manly Christianity. He used to say "remember boys, when we put off the old man we must not put on the old woman!" Evenings such as this often went on into the wee small hours and T.S. was never keen to draw them to a close — he seemed to have unending stamina.

On one occasion, unknown to him of course, a few of his seniors decided to try and outsit him around the fire. The chat was good and they felt at 3.00 a.m. that they were doing well, but, at 3.30 a.m., when T.S. said "put on another shovelful of coal, boys, the fire is getting a bit low", they decided that it was time to surrender and return home!

These evenings are fondly remembered by Crusaders for they realise what a privilege it was to have the benefit of T.S.'s great spiritual wisdom. They realise that it was on such occasions that he encouraged them to start coming to Leaders' Conferences or to offer their services as officers at Camp or House Party, and thus begin to make the transition from being members of the Class to being leaders. It is no coincidence that a high percentage of the Seniors who have gone through the Londonderry Class are now involved in the leadership of a number of other Crusader Classes throughout the Union.

In recent years, as more and more Crusaders sought their university education across the Irish Sea, T.S. realised the importance of keeping in touch with them. Every Crusader who travelled thus, discovered that a letter from their leader was awaiting their arrival to cheer them up and to give them the sound advice which was contained in this letter to a student at Lancaster University in 1974, "the important thing is to establish contact with the Inter-Varsity Fellowship group in the University, for there you are more likely to make Christian friends, and that is terribly important, for the stand a fellow takes at the start is likely to colour his whole university career. 'Well begun is half done' applies to this with a very special relevance. "This was the first of some 30 letters this student received from Mr. Mooney during his University career — all signed "yours Crusaderly".

T.S. also used his wide network of contacts to ensure that his Crusaders settled in well at University. One could quote dozens of examples, but space permits only two. A student at Nottingham University writes "before I went, he wrote to the Professor of Bio-chemistry, a local Crusader leader, to see if he would welcome me. He did, and it certainly helped me to find my feet." A student at Dundee remembers that T.S. visited him just a few days after he started university, "Mr. Mooney introduced me to the local minister and I attended his Church throughout my University career."

As he prayed regularly for his Crusader students and wrote to them often, it was only natural that he should be keen to see them on their return home when term ended. His happy knack of knowing when they would is best expressed by one student who said, "he had an almost paranormal ability to detect one's imminent return during university vacations."

On these evenings when notes were compared on the activities of the various Christian Unions, the usual fare of Campbell's soup, fairly thick in texture because T.S. always insisted on diluting it with milk instead of water, toast, cheese and Lily's famous boiled cake tasted all the nicer for one felt that one was really home again.

T.S. will not just be remembered for his prayerful and pastoral concern for boys, vital though they may be. He will also be remembered as a marvellous Bible Teacher who had the ability to bring the Book to life in a manner which the boys found relevant and attractive. Using "alliteration's artful aid" and a wide variety of apt illustrations, culled from wide reading in his extensive library, together with his great command of the English language, he was greatly used of God as he sought in a definite, but unemotional, way to encourage the boys to put their trust in the Saviour whom he loved. A couple of talks spring to mind. Speaking of Noah's Ark as a way of salvation he noted that it was a *suitable* way of salvation, a *scorned way* of salvation and a *sole* way of salvation. When speaking of manna as the bread of life for the Children of Israel in the desert he noted that they received it early in the day, they received it every day and they received it to the end of their days.

Many would say that he was at his best at evening prayers at the Castlerock Camp. One Crusader leader with over 20 years experience recalls his boyhood memories thus: "How he kept us so fully attentive at the end of a day's activities, sitting in a hot room, can only be explained in terms of the power of the Spirit through the Word. I still remember the impact of his talk over 30 years ago on the text 'And sitting down they watched Him there' as, in imagination, he enabled us to enter the thoughts of those who sat around the Cross."

The same leader goes on to say "he had a profound influence on my life. I only saw him about 10 days a year as a teenager, at Camp and House Party, but that was enough. He was a single-minded representative of His Lord, not the harrassed frantic, fanatical sort, but rather the type who knows what he had been called to do and has time to do it; and so he moved through life as one of those 'whose ordered lives confess the beauty of Thy peace' ".

T.S. was unique. He was a one off. We shall never see his like again for, when the Lord made T.S., he broke the mould. We in Crusaders thank God for every remembrance of him and surely our prayer for the future could be expressed no better than in the words of John Wesley on hearing of George Whitfield's death in 1770 "May the rising generation catch a spark of the flame which shone with such distinguished lustre in the spirit and practice of this faithful servant of the Most High God."

John Magowan

MOONEYISMS

No man was ever the worse mentally, morally or spiritually for being a total abstainer but the name is legion of those who came to grief through their failure to be so. There are times when it is well worth while to be 'odd man out' for no total abstainer ever became an alcoholic.

Holiday idleness has its dangers . . . The Master's warning, "Watch and Pray", is never more necessary than when in new surroundings we are tempted to forget old loyalties.

Some people go to church as if to the dentist, and return looking as if they had been there. If that cynicism is true, what a contrast we are to the first century Christians for it was said of them that they outlived, outloved, and outlaughed the pagans.

A small boy, who enjoyed a summer Crusader camp so well, explained why to his parents when he got home by saying, "You know, the great thing about Mr. Mooney is that he isn't a bit religious."

The great task of the church is not only to get sinners into heaven, but also to get saints out of bed.

GREATHEART

The Guide who kept the Pilgrims wise about the snares set for their feet

Now I saw in my dream that they went on until they were come to the place that Simple, and Sloth, and Presumption lay and slept in, when Christian went by on pilgrimage; and behold, they were hanged up in irons a little way off on the other side.

Then said Mercy to Greatheart who was their Guide and Conductor, "What are these three men? and for what are they hanged there?"

And Greatheart said "These three men were men of very bad qualities; they had no mind to be pilgrims themselves, and whomsoever they could they hindered. They were for sloth and folly themselves and whomsoever they could persuade they made so too; and withal taught them to presume that they should do well at last; and, now you go by, they are hanged."

Next he showed them the two byways that were at the foot of the hill (Difficulty) where Formality and Hypocrisy lost themselves. And he said, "These are dangerous paths."

Then said Greatheart to the boys, "Come, my boys, how do you do? What think you now of going on pilgrimage?" "Sir, said the youngest, I was almost beat out of heart but I thank you for lending me a hand in my need."

CHAPTER THREE

The Friend of Students

Having accepted the invitation of those who planned this symposium on the life and work of Thomas Smyth Mooney to write this chapter on his friendships, and his influence with students, I am glad to do so as a tribute to one who as my Sunday School teacher, Bible Class leader and student guide, was also my very true friend for almost sixty years. It may be that some who, like myself, were students at Magee University College, Londonderry and who entered the ministry of the Church, or perhaps went into teaching, will remember, and be inspired, I hope, by some of the things which I recall. I hope they will also recapture some of the joy which we found in fellowship with one whom we affectionately knew as "T.S."

At one time in his life, as he himself has said, T.S. had hoped to study for the ministry of the Presbyterian Church in Ireland, but after narrowly missing a university scholarship which would have taken him there, he sat the Entrance examination for the Belfast Banking Co. and passed with such high distinction (second place in Northern Ireland) that he felt this was a clear indication of his calling in life. Although he did not enter the ministry of his own beloved Church it became clear that he was chosen to serve his Lord in another unique way, namely, by influencing and encouraging students not only of his own Church but of other Churches as well, and those who entered other professions too.

Living as he did most of his life in Londonderry he had the opportunity of meeting and befriending many of the students attending Magee University College. He drafted them into the Londonderry Crusader Class and offered them the experience of working with boys as Junior officers in the Class and at the Northern Ireland Crusader Camps. This became for many an invaluable training ground for Christian service. When he conducted church services on Sundays in many different congregations he often asked students for the ministry to accompany him. He would invite them to lead the service or to give the talk to the children, and afterwards he discussed with them the conduct of a Presbyterian service. One thing which I recall now is that he never allowed the devotional part of the service to be dismissed as the 'preliminaries'. It is, therefore, about his influence and encouragement in this and other ways that I have been asked to write. I fondly remember him as an 'encourager of students'.

Although he left school at eighteen years of age he remained a student all his life. His library was packed with books — shelves upon shelves of them — and he knew them. He had a wonderful collection of theological 'classics', James Denney, Alexander Whyte, W. M. Clow, Andrew Bonar and other worthies being among his favourites. He picked up second-hand books wherever he went in Northern Ireland or in Scotland, and many men received a parcel of books with the note, "You may find these useful; look up particularly at a certain chapter in such and such a book."

He kept up-to-date with modern theological thinking and he perused a wide variety of weekly and monthly magazines from various Churches and Missionary Societies. His interest in Church History and particularly that of Scotland and its Kirk; also his love of Christian biography, all 'rubbed off' on many students. They marvelled at the way he could draw illustrations from the 'saints' of all ages. When he visited my manse for a brief holiday or to conduct a service in the Church, he would run his finger along the books on the shelves and if he came across a book he had not read he would pick it up, and if he did not think it worth reading he would put it down quickly again and pass on to another. Sometimes he would take one or two books to his bedroom and have them read in the morning. He was gifted with a most retentive memory. He could read books quickly and yet remember what he had read. He had a rare knack of quoting accurately from them and of applying the quotation at the right time and place. By his wide and varied reading, and his awareness of other theological positions, as well as his sometimes ruthless demolition of them when he thought they were wrong, he gave added weight, as far as students were concerned, to his own well-reasoned and well-articulated convictions and beliefs.

He often insisted that he would not waste too much of his time reading anything but 'conservative' theology, yet at the time of the controversy over Bishop A. T. Robinson's book, "Honest to God", he amazed those of us who discussed it with him by his knowledge of the wide range of opinions, both those who agreed with what Robinson was trying to do and those who disagreed. Being obviously so well read, and possessing such a phenomenal memory, he was at home in any company.

In his study which was lined with many photographs of former Crusaders and student friends (which he jocularly called the 'Rogues' Gallery') he could discourse at length on most theological subjects and with ease. He would often probe with a few telling questions and then sit back and listen. Then he would dissect what he had heard and he could sum up most discussions with a few memorable and telling phrases. His store of anecdotes and stories appropriate to the occasion and to the discussion seemed to be inexhaustible, and came from his wide and varied reading, and his patient observations of human nature and life.

In the Crusader Class his talks were often in series and some of these were memorable; "Bible Characters", "The Acts of the Apostles", and "Great doctrines of the Faith", come easily to mind for they were faithfully expounded in such an interesting and racy manner, with more than a touch of humour, and well illustrated with interesting stories that even the younger boys could follow and understand. What solid Bible teaching was being given! and what solid foundations were being laid! Moreover, what times of fellowship and prayer were enjoyed in what he called the "Keenites", which was a meeting for further Bible study during the week. Without a doubt they laid a sure foundation of good things in the spiritual development of many boys. In prayer he used simple but telling phrases with many Biblical quotations, especially from the Psalms, and while so fluent they were equally full of meaning and power, and were remembered and appreciated by all of us who were privileged to hear them.

His influence on students attending Magee University College was as remarkable as it was unique. He had that great gift of making you feel that you were important to him as a person. From time to time, through seemingly casual conversation, or by letter, for he was a great letter-writer, he encouraged many students by a genuine interest in their studies or in their work

21

when they were ordained. Often he wrote short letters, thanking people for little kindnesses, for their hospitality, for attending the Crusader Birthday service or for sending a message of greeting; and he had always something encouraging to write.

On the first occasion he heard me preach in our home congregation of Great James Street, Londonderry, (and it was with some trepidation I did so when I knew that he was present in the congregation) he wrote to me afterwards,

"To hear you preach the truth of the Gospel of Jesus Christ made my heart thrill; and to know that you were a former member of my Crusader Class made my heart rejoice."

Truly, there are many more who could say, of T.S. what Paul wrote of Onesiphorus, in 2 Tim. 1:16 "Many a time did he put fresh heart in me." (Goodspeed's Trans.) To know that you were on his Prayer List was a steadying influence and a tremendous help.

To the many who sought his advice he was a friend and counsellor extraordinary; they never left him without hearing something to their advantage. If someone wrote to him for help, they were sure of a letter by return of post. Many a raw young student, unsure of his theological position, was invited by T.S. for supper and the discussion lasted into the "wee sma' hours". One of our ministers told me how he discussed the liberal criticism of the Genesis story of Creation which he had come across from other students and from some College professors. T.S. went through his Bible, indicating the veracity of the Scriptures, and convicted by what he heard, that minister came away and never again doubted the truth of God's Word. The impact of that interview remained with him all through his ministry.

Many a student, including myself, sought his advice when troubled about the difficulties associated with the doctrine and practice of Baptism. Patiently with his Bible open and turning from one passage to another he expounded his view of "Covenant theology" and settled the many doubts that plagued us. I fervently hope that the talk which I heard him give on "Infant Baptism" at the Evangelical Union will be found among his notes and published; it would be a great help in these days when the question of what a credible profession of faith means worries so many people.

22

When they had to deal with awkward people in difficult situations many sought his advice. He often said it was better to laugh with people and at them than to become entangled with matters of little importance. "Save your energies for the big battles of the Faith," he would say. Nevertheless where there was a genuine problem involved he was never afraid to speak his mind and he gave sound, common-sense advice based on his wide experience of Christian work.

He could be devastating in his criticism, and some who heard him speak thus felt the lash of his wit and sarcasm; he felt so strongly about spiritual matters that at times he could scarce contain himself. Yet he was kind and considerate to any who were really seeking help and advice. Perhaps it was because he had no patience with cant and hypocrisy that he appeared at times to speak so sharply.

The consuming passion of his work among students was that they should be 'ambassadors for Christ' in the Church, in the teaching profession, or wherever they might be called to serve. To know Jesus Christ in a living and personal way and to lead others to know Him as Saviour and Lord was the purpose of all his living. He himself never ceased to be thrilled with the wonder of the Gospel, with the power of the Name of Jesus and of the truth of the Word of God. Because it thrilled him he longed that all should proclaim the same message with the same purpose and power.

He accepted many preaching engagements and wherever he went his ministry of the Word was greatly appreciated and blessed. He was described by some as "the finest lay preacher in the Presbyterian Church." Certainly his style and manner in the pulpit commended the Gospel truth he loved to proclaim. As one man said in my hearing, "If there were more men like that in the pulpit, there would be more men like me in the pews."

He was a "High Churchman" in the best sense of the term and he exhorted all students for the ministry of the Church to be the same. He constantly exhorted them to be fervently evangelical and loyally denominational, and strictly in that order.

It is worth recalling words which he wrote in the *Presbyterian Herald* (Nov. 1978) on "What sort of society do we want?"; they exemplify in essence his belief and what he sought to inculcate in others.

23

"The society that I want to see is based on the Christian home, where the kindly discipline of 'Children, obey your parents' replaces the modern idea of 'Parents, obey your children, and deny them nothing for which they ask, lest they feel frustrated and suffer psychological damage." Naturally, wise parents will not nag continually at their children but, remembering their own youth and being mindful of the fact of original Sin, they won't expect too much of their boys and girls. The home I want to see is one where kindly discipline combined with reasonable liberty ensures that youngsters who might have developed into likeable and attractive folk don't become spoiled brats. *"It is a wise saying that 'the family that prays together stays together' and this applies not merely to prayers offered around the fireside but to those that ascend from the family pew. The society I want is one where children are not sent to church but taken there by parents whose loyalty to the house of God is never in question and whose Sunday dinner table-talk is never a criticism or a 'debunking' of the service or the sermon."*

"If, however, this is to be true, the Church has its own part to play. The minister must have something worthwhile to say and have learned the art of getting it across to the congregation. He must not have earned the reputation of a certain American preacher that 'he could dive the deepest, stay under the longest and come up the driest of any preacher in town.' " His prayers must be earnest rather than eloquent, and the praise must be such as a congregation will love to sing. I want to see a Church where people love each other and are not ashamed to show it openly, who warmly welcome a visitor at a service so that whenever they meet a stranger they leave a friend. In spite of their love and loyalty to their own congregation and denomination they will still have a place in their hearts for all who love Christ. This will not mean that they are ardent ecumenists but that, while they cherish their own strong convictions, they have learned to disagree without being disagreeable.

"I want to see a Church that will send out into the world of business and economics a stream of men, whether employers or employees, whose hearts the Lord has touched and who in their daily work will remember that they also have a Master in heaven. If the Christian Church is to be true to itself then even in such a situation as we face in Northern Ireland she must never despair. The Church has two resources peculiar to herself, namely, the power of Christ's Gospel and the power of the Holy Spirit, plus men and women who have been savingly influenced thereby."

"I want to see a Church enthusiastically preaching that Gospel that 1900 years ago was reputed to have turned the world upside down, and to see that Gospel by the power of the Spirit producing church members who will take its message to their fellows and whose lives will be a convincing testimony to its power. That, of course, would be a religious revival, and such a movement would leave its mark on every part of our social, political, and business life. Did not a secular historian say of a movement of that sort in the eighteenth century that 'only the revival under the Wesleys saved England from revolution? The society that I want to see is one that is the product of such a revival.' "

Such an influence as is reflected in this article is the influence that T.S. had upon generations of students and it has remained with many of them right to this day. In correspondence and in conversation they still recall his words of wisdom and not least his memorable "quotes" which he loved so much. Some of them were original and some were from the writers he loved but they have never been forgotten through the years by those men he encouraged and inspired on their Christian pilgrimage, and who even to-day thank God on every remembrance of him.

Two of the "quotes", already mentioned spring to mind and as they are not unrelated to the topic of this chapter we recall them here:

★ Thomas Chalmers, the first principal of New College, Edinburgh used to say to his class of theological students, "Gentlemen, when you enter the pulpit, don't be ashamed to be known as men of one commodity, namely salvation through a justifying faith in the precious blood of the Lamb."

★ Never despise the Church, Never despair of the Church. Never desert the Church.

Eric M. Borland

MOONEYISMS

The important thing is not the kind of office to which you ordain a man, but the kind of man that you ordain to the office.

An ardent and uncompromising loyalty on the part of both the Church of Ireland and the Presbyterian Church in Ireland to the apostolic Gospel as summarised in the Thirty Nine Articles and in the Westminister Confession of Faith would do more to further Church Unity than many conferences and octaves.

GREATHEART
A brother and friend to all God's people

GREATHEART: *Come, Mr. Feeble-mind, pray you go along with us. I will be your conductor and you will fare as the rest.*

FEEBLE-MIND: *Alas, I need a suitable companion . . . I do not know all the truth; I am a very ignorant Christian man. Sometimes if I hear any rejoice in the Lord, it troubles me because I cannot do so too. It is with me as it is with a weak man among the strong, or as a sick man among the healthy.*

GREATHEART: *But brother, I have it in commission to comfort the feeble-minded and to support the weak. You must go along with us; we will wait for you. We will lend you our help; we will deny ourselves of some things, opinionative and practical, for your sake. We will not enter into doubtful disputations before you. We will be made all things to you, rather than you shall be left behind.*

CHAPTER FOUR

For Christ and the Church

"A brother in Christ!" When I use those words about T. S. Mooney I am doing so because I believe that no higher tribute can be paid by one man to another than to say just that; and T.S. was that and far more than that to me.

I was called to the congregation of Gt. James St. Presbyterian Church, Londonderry in 1947 and even then he was a valued member of the congregation there. Throughout my years among that lovable people T.S. stood out in a unique way, a brother and a friend in every respect. He was a man of practical, business-like efficiency and confidence, but an overbearing attitude was foreign to him. All his many gifts he carried with grace and humility. It was only when requested that he would give advice or guidance on matters affecting the pulpit inside it or out. Moreover, he had such a courteous and honest way of expressing his opinions that no hint of captious criticism was ever left behind. I owe him more than I can ever express.

Of course, when it came to debate and discussion around the fireside it was different. Then time did not matter; he might drop in for supper and it might be one o'clock in the morning before he left. Yet he was up invariably before anyone else for he lived a disciplined life which was only known by those who were close to him. He used to say (quoting, I think, a famous Scottish Professor,) that if a minister were to be found in his bedroom slippers at 10 a.m. he was in a dangerous state of soul, and unworthy to be a minister of Christ's gospel. Nevertheless those hours of sharing were unforgettable. His pithy comments, his humorous acecdotes and the quotations and references from his wide reading could never go unremembered, and then to end all, his prayers so plain and Scriptural.

For most of his life he was a member of the Kirk Session and took an active part in all its work and deliberations. Patiently he would listen to what others had to say before he made any comment and what he had to add was succinct and to the point.

27

His tact and humour settled many an issue happily when it seemed certain to cause division. At one meeting the Session were discussing the matter of how the offering was received at the Sunday services. The stewards had been accustomed to taking the plates back with them to their own pews and placing them on the floor underneath their seats till the end of the service. There was some evidence that some were for 'no change' but when T.S. had the opportunity to speak he said, "I think we must be ashamed of what we put on the plates . . ." "Why so?" he was asked. "Well", he said, "we sit on them and hide them." When asked for his suggestions he went on, "Could we not go about that part of our worship in a decent and orderly fashion and leave our gifts on a table at the front of the church." It solved a problem which perhaps should never have arisen but which was capable of rousing feelings.

In any evaluation of T. S. Mooney it must never be forgotten that he loved his Church and was completely loyal to her. He delighted to worship 'in simple form as Presbyterians do'. The old metrical psalms were a strong part of his devotional life and he loved to quote them, yes, and sing them, although he was not much of a singer. He welcomed any opportunity of becoming part of the wider circle of evangelical work and witness but he never strayed far from his Covenanting background. His shelves were filled with the volumes of "The Old Scots Worthies" and he loved to say, quoting the late Rev. Prof. R. L. Marshall's words at the Tercentenary of the Presbyterian Church in Ireland, that "our tap roots stretched across the heather and the centuries to a hill outside a city wall."

As an elder he was most faithful in all his duties. No matter what his other commitments may have been he seldom missed a meeting. In his district he was highly respected and as a representative elder at Presbytery, or later at the General Assembly, he followed every discussion with knowledge and insight. Whenever he went to the rostrum to speak he was given the House's full attention and deep respect. He sat on many committees and boards, and represented the Church at wider Christian gatherings. People did not always accept his views any more than he accepted theirs, but even when that was the case he could never be disagreeable. There was nothing small or petty about him for he was large in mind and in heart.

One of the outstanding things about Tom Mooney was his influence with and upon young people. For many years the congregation had him as a teacher in the Sunday School and Bible Class. He had great gifts as a teacher and his Bible Class talks were clear and lucid. The Shorter Catechism was also an indispensable part of his Bible Class programme, and again and again he found the answer to many a theological difficulty in that noble little manual. Christian Endeavour also claimed his loyalty for he saw in that organisation an excellent means of winning folk for Christ, and training them in intelligent and efficent service for Christ and the Church.

So far as he himself was concerned his preparation for speaking or writing was meticulous. To have seen some of his papers and notes was an education in how such things should be done. His many articles for our congregational magazine were worthy of a larger readership and especially memorable were the notes he wrote about the Lord's Supper, the Church of Christ and the celebration of Christmas. It is to be hoped that some of these will be preserved.

Another part of Church work which he seemed to make his own was the proposing of a vote of thanks, especially to the ladies on the occasion of a supper. No Annual meeting of the congregation at Gt. James St. seemed to be complete without his final appearance on the platform, no matter what other business he had presented before that, and usually this speech was the highlight of the evening. He was known to have said on more than one such occasion that while he was strongly of the opinion that the ladies should be given the right hand of fellowship, he as a bachelor believed in keeping them at arm's length.

He had a tremendous gift of speech and a felicitous use of language that was always clear and simple. "No padding and nothing flowery" seemed to be his motto. To all this he added a great repertoire of stories and incidents, all of which were made to add point to what he had to say. Then, it was often remarked that he very seldom finished a speech without saying a good word for his Lord and Master.

He had many invitations to local pulpits especially in the country districts and there he was assured of a warm welcome. His sermons never failed to get an attentive hearing and were often remembered and rehearsed by the congregation elsewhere.

One such sermon of his was often gleefully recalled and repeated by those who heard it. It was a harvest service and Mr. Mooney had preached on "The Sower went forth to sow." He spoke of the seed that never got IN, then of the seed that got in but never got DOWN. Then there was the seed that got in, and got down, but never got UP, and finally he spoke of the seed that got in, and got down, and then got up and got OUT. Is it any wonder that the people heard T.S. gladly when he came to preach to them?

It goes almost without saying that he was much involved in the Christian witness within the city of Londonderry. The City Mission, the Christian Workers Union and the Temperance movement were all there when he went and he supported them with vigour and enthusiasm. Anything that was for the Christian good of Derry had his support, and if the salvation of men's souls was involved he never held back no matter who made the first move. The Young People's Convention, which has just celebrated its fiftieth cenvention was his own creation, and of course his Crusader Class, of which others can speak more fully that I can, also began under his leadership.

That introduces the matter of his influence with schoolboys and students. Here, again, someone else will speak but I may comment about those who belonged to my congregation; they would never willingly have missed a Sunday afternoon at 'Crusaders'. Very many of them could trace back their life in Christ to what they heard, learned and believed there. It is arguable that no other similar Christian body was responsible for sending so many men into the Christian ministry at home and overseas, — and they were not all Presbyterians by any means — as that old class up in the Diamond. It was and has remained 'holy ground' for very many. His correspondence from all over the world and from men at every level of public, professional and social life is indicative of the value of that work. It must not be thought that this work was more or less the natural impact of a strong personality on impressionable youth; nothing could be further from the truth than that. The influence of T.S. was in no way emotional or sensational. Based on the clear teaching of Scripture, and presented in his own magnetic way, the class enjoyed the blessing of the Holy Spirit to an extraordinary degree. At the same time he did not make the Christian life an easy option for anyone. His appeals for decision for Christ did not hide the sternness of the upward climb involved, and the amazing thing was that all that was manly arose in them as they committed themselves for life to the Saviour Who died for them.

His interest in the Kingdom of God did not stop at Londonderry and his membership of the Council of the Qua Iboe Mission was indicative of his deep interest and effort for the work of the Kingdom of God in other lands. When the Mission sent him to visit the field and the churches of the Qua Iboe Church Fellowship it made a deep impression upon him and was the culmination of a lifetime's interest. He was, to the very last, an intelligent supporter and liberal contributor to many different societies while never neglecting that of his own Church.

Like the 'men of the Covenant' of whom he often spoke and whom he held in high esteem, T.S. related little of his own Christian experience. He talked much of his home and of his early school days; also of his boyhood's church, Dromore Original Secession congregation, and of his conversion too. Nevertheless he was reluctant to enter into any detailed discussion about his subsequent spiritual pilgrimage. He would drop hints now and then and like many of those 'fathers' whom he respected so much he displayed a humble reticence. Nevertheless we all knew that he was a man 'far ben with God'. His love for and longing toward that deeper spiritual life was evidenced by his life-long support of the Portstewart Convention. As a student I never forget his nightly visit to the students' camp where he shared supper and in his own way brought a discussion round to the addresses given in the tent that evening.

As a businessman in the city he won the respect of a wide circle of commercial leaders. It was an open secret that he could easily have risen to a high position in his profession if he had wanted to leave Londonderry with all its Church and Crusaders interests but this he did not want to do. As it was he became pro-manager of the Londonderry branch of the Belfast Banking Co. and for many years enjoyed the esteem of many who had business there. As in everything else he was direct and clear with as much kindly attention for those who had small accounts as for those with large ones; it was always the individual person that mattered to him.

In writing all this I am only echoing what my predecessors, the

31

Very Rev. Dr. James Thompson, the Rev. J. A. Donaldson and my successor too, Very Rev. Dr. George Wynne would have said again and again. He was to them all, all that he proved to be to me. His later years saw the removal of Gt. James St. Church over the river to Kilfennan. In many ways it was a sad experience for those who loved the old meeting house and T.S. mourned over it with everybody else. Nevertheless as soon as the decision was taken and the new congregation erected he gave his full support to the work and to the new minister, the Rev. Edgar McKinney. No one was more delighted to see the work of the Spirit in the new area than he was. No one rejoiced more over the large attendances and the conversions which were the fruit of that work than he did. He had a great respect for the congregation's storied past but he also gave the new Church all the support he could. "Hats off to the past; coats off for the future." That was indeed his habit.

An old lady once called the saintly Professor Henry Drummond to the bedside of her dying husband. "He'll no hear ye for he's deaf," she said, "and he'll no see ye for he's blind. But I want him to have a breath o' ye afore he dies." T. S. Mooney was a man of similar spirit. He brought not only truth but also grace and loveliness of character with it. There was an atmosphere when he was around that came from a very close walk with God.

The prophet Malachi prophesied to a decadent leadership among the people of Israel and he reminded them that the original covenant which God made was with a different type of man altogether. It is so like the slim, sharp, saintly figure of T. S. Mooney of Londonderry who kept a whole community wholesome, proud to be a Derry man and prouder still to be a humble servant of the Lord Jesus Christ. Here is the portrait in words simple and plain like himself:

"He feared Me and stood in awe of My name. True instruction was in his mouth and no wrong was found in his life. He walked with Me in peace and uprightness and he turned many from iniquity". (Mal. 2:5-6).

That was T. S. Mooney — A brother beloved!

David Burke

32

Gt. James Street Presbyterian Church 1837—1982

★ *The congregation was founded in 1834 and was known as "Scots Kirk". The building was opened in 1837.*

★ *Four of its ministers became Moderators of General Assembly and one declined nomination.*

★ *Owing to the movement of the Protestant popultion to the Waterside area the congregation was transplanted there and became 'Kilfennan' in 1982.*

★ *A N.I. Tourist Board leaflet, dealing with the churches of Londonderry described Gt. James Street Church as having "the most elegant interior of the city churches". Mr. Mooney thought so too and was proud of it but, in his next issue of the "Messenger" he also recalled a famous Scottish preacher, Dr. Norman Maclean of Skye who said, "It is not carved pillars and groined roofs that make a church beautiful; it is the prayers and praises of the living congregation." That was why T.S. led the move with the people to Kilfennan.*

★   *1978/79.   Decision taken to move to Kilfennan.*

★   *Jan. 1980.   Plans finalised for Kilfennan Church.*

★   *Mar. 1980.   Authority given to sell the Gt. James Street Property.*

★   *4 April 1982   The Rev. Edgar S. McKinney, Dip.Th., B.D. installed.*

★   *5 Sept. 1982.   The last service in Gt. James Street.*

★   *11 Sept. 1982.   The new church officially opened by Very Rev. Dr. John Girvan.*

★   *12 Sept. 1982.   The first services in Kilfennan were conducted by Rev. Edgar S. McKinney.*

MOONEYISMS

Three things are necessary from every Church member — love, loyalty and labour "— and the greatest of these is love", for if it is present, the other two will certainly follow.

CHAPTER FIVE

T.S.: The Minister's Man

I feel ill-equipped to write this chapter about the life of Mr. T. S. Mooney. There are many ministers throughout the General Assembly who knew Mr. Mooney far better than I did. Each could write volumes about this undoubtedly great man. Many ministers could record their indebtedness to his wisdom in the area of spiritual matters. My qualification is that I had the privilege of being the last minister under whom Mr. Mooney sat. However, I lay claim to one other qualification. When I arrived in Londonderry in April 1982, it was to face the challenge of a church just about to move its centre of work and witness from the "Cityside" to the "Waterside" of Londonderry. I came to this task a relatively inexperienced minister, so I leant heavily on the experienced members of Kirk Session who prayerfully surrounded me. Chief among my advisors was Mr. Mooney. Therefore I believe I can rightly claim that few ministers have been more helped and blessed by the ministry of "T.S." than I have.

He was a rather shy man, but one who wouldn't allow that to inhibit his formation of friendships. We were thrown together by the unusual circumstances of Gt. James Street Presbyterian Church. We quickly formed a close relationship which would only be inadequately defined as friendship. Our home became his home and our table, his. How my wife loved to see him come! He never complained no matter what was set before him; so long as there was an adequate supply of salt and pepper, he had no complaints. My children's only criticism was that he stayed too short a time and too much of his time was spent talking to Daddy. He had a unique way with kids; they noted the sincerity that lay behind all the interesting questions that were asked. Perhaps it was relaxed humour that helped him form such instant friendships with all children. Never would he leave the house without the courtesy of thanking my wife ("Ma'am" rather than Sandra) for "her hospitality". His death was a blow for all my family, for us it was the passing of a friend. For my children he was the grandfather figure who will never be replaced. He was more than the minister's man — he was the minister's friend.

He came to Londonderry in 1925 and remained a most loyal member of the congregation until his death almost sixty-one years later. In a congregation of such long-standing traditions as Gt. James Street, it was unusual, if not unique, for such a "young man" from outside the City to be so prematurely elected to the high office of elder. In 1943 Mr. Mooney was ordained an elder. His unanimous election to the position of Clerk of Session in 1971 was one which was humbly and reluctantly accepted. He served three ministers in this capacity: the late Very Rev. Dr. George Wynne, the Rev. William McBride Campbell, now minister in Legacurry Presbyterian Church, and myself. His annual holiday to Strathpeffer in Scotland was the only interruption to his faithfulness in church life. There was nothing unusual in Mr. Mooney leaving a Board Meeting in Church House, Belfast, to drive the seventy-five miles to Londonderry to be present at the Kirk Session Meeting only to return to Belfast early the next morning to attend another Board Meeting. There was a rare faithfulness about this man! He would not allow any obstacle to stand in his way of serving Christ in the Church. What a delight for any minister to know that the first to arrive at the Prayer Meeting or the Midweek Fellowship would be his clerk of Session. In the life of the Church he indeed was the minister's man.

When I heard other ministers talk about the complaints and criticisms which can originate with their Clerks of Session, I was forced to thank God for mine. Not only was Mr. Mooney hesitant to criticise his own minister but he was also quick to stifle any criticism from others of "their minister". Did this attitude originate from too lofty a view of the role of the minister? I think not! It came from a gracious attitude towards everyone. He was by nature a person who sought to praise the good and, therefore, he had no time to find fault. Yet there was no trace of naivety about this man, his ministry was one of positive encouragement rather than negative criticism. How encouraging it was to have him as my Clerk of Session. He was oil on troubled water as he sought to see the other person's point of view. Frequently I looked to him for advice and, on occasions, consolation and encouragement. His knowledge of the church was refreshingly

36

up to date. His Code was read for guidance and his Bible for inspiration. So the advice I received was always Biblical and technically correct. The warmth of the man came from the intimacy of his relationship with Christ. Perhaps it was my admiration, if not envy, for his personal spiritual qualities that attracted me to seek out his wisdom. I must have frustrated him with my questions, yet his patience with me was not unique for many other young ministers share in my testimony to his patience. He was more than the minister's man — he was the minister's pastor.

Perhaps I have given the impression that this great man was so spiritual that he could not see the realities and pressures of the minister's life. That would be quite unfair, for no-one could have had a more sympathetic supporter than I found in Mr. Mooney. Despite being a bachelor he had an acute awareness of the pressures which can come upon any family and especially upon the Manse family. He quietly persuaded me to pursue sporting interests so that the body might be equipped for the service of the Lord as well as the soul. Shortly after I had taken up my duties in Londonderry he arrived unannounced at our door to find me just about to leave the house for a round of golf. I was slightly apprehensive about what the great T. S. Mooney might think of his minister indulging in such a "worldly" pastime as golf. Far from criticising, I found myself encouraged to go on ahead, as he was passing by later on and could quite easily call back. This concern for me was quite typical of the man. His experience came to the fore when, through no fault of my own, pressures of work were in danger of overwhelming me. In the next Kirk Session Meeting he unashamedly seized the initiative and suggested that the minister needed a week free from duties. On my return from a week's holiday I felt considerably refreshed, so much so that even I could see how exhausted I had been. He was a good barometer for me, an amber warning light about how well I was coping with the stress and the workload. He had the spiritual welfare of the minister at heart, but also he had an acute concern for the Man of God. Indeed it would be true to say he was the Minister's Man.

By the time Mr. Mooney and I forged our team ministry he was already well into his seventies. One might have expected him to have been a rather traditional and conservative thinker. Nothing could be further from the truth! He was a conservative evangelical in his theology but that was the only way in which he was conservative. He survived several crises in the seventies: the unexpected death of his great friend, the Very Rev. Dr. George Wynne in his Moderatorial year, was a heartbreak for him. His own major heart surgery shortly afterwards left him weakened for a time. The arrival of the enthusiastic Rev. William Campbell saw a new era opening up for Gt. James Street . . . or so it seemed. Yet Mr. Mooney was ever the realist to see that the pattern of decline would only be temporarily arrested, no matter how enthusiastic the minister. How greatly the whole congregation benefited from his counsel at the time of their taking that traumatic decision to close their church and move to a new site on the Waterside at Kilfennan. When Mr. Campbell was called to take up a chaplaincy in the Army the spiritual leadership was found in the Clerk of Session. It is a tribute to him that Kilfennan opened in September 1982 as a happy and united congregation.

Although his love of Gt. James Street never decreased, he didn't allow it to be an obstacle in his new enthusiasm for Kilfennan. The crowd of new faces was greeted with his winning smile and enthusiasm for the "new church". New converts were a constant source of delight to him; what encouragement they found in his enthusiastic reception of them. There were frequent invitations to supper and once the "iron stairway" had been mounted, the chat was rich and encouraging. With a new building and the influx of new members, Mr. Mooney was one of the first to suggest that these new members ought to be given areas of responsibility and leadership. His example was followed by many, and so forestalled any possibility of an "us" and "them" mentality ever forming. In him the old and young were beautifully combined. His maturity in the faith and his enthusiasm about new ideas, brought a most necessary binding force to the whole church.

In one way, perhaps more than any other, he was the minister's man — in the area of prayer. His prayer life was the envy of all who knew him. How often I've found myself saying that I will pray for a particular person, only to be guilty of infrequently keeping my pledge. Very soon after meeting the famous T. S. Mooney I became aware that this was no straw hero in the faith. Here was a truly great man, a man of God. The secret of his power was the presence of Christ in his life. Behind this quiet confidence in the faith was a humility and humble confidence in the power of prayer. How often have we found it to be true that behind a great man of God we will find a great prayer life. This was certainly true of Mr. Mooney.

Until I met him I always thought the frequent references Paul made to praying for "everyone", "all the time" was probably only an expression which meant that he was frequently praying for them. Now I have discovered a whole new world of prayer, for I've met and been prayed for by a man who took the command to "pray always" to be an attainable goal. I have the privilege of being one of those for whom Mr. Mooney prayed every day. Oh how I praise God for that source of power in my life. In the solitude of his bedroom and on his knees with his "diary of prayer" spread out before him, this was where he got his spirituality from. That daily contact with God blessed many ministries. Perhaps it would be more accurate to call him a "ministers' man" rather than a "minister's man". He sustained many and did so through his prayer life.

His attendance at our Prayer Meeting has already been missed, his eloquence and sincerity were perfectly blended. Those who were new in the faith had an example to follow; those who were mature in the faith had a new target to aim at. My life is impoverished by his death and my ministry is a little less effective because of the absence of his prayer life. I wonder if yours is the same! Maybe there is a need for each of us to take up the challenge of his intercessory prayer life. I acknowledge his impact on my ministry. For me he wasn't just the minister's man but the man in my ministry. I praise God for him!

Edgar S. McKinney

MOONEYISM

You cannot have fire in the pulpit if you have icebergs in the pews.

GREATHEART

The Guide who, to make the way safer for others, took on all
sorts of enemies himself

*Then said the GIANT MAUL, "How many times have you, Mr.
Great-Heart, been forbidden to do these things . . . I will put an end to
your trade. Thou practisest the trade of a kidnapper; thou carriest
them away into a strange country, to the weakening of my master's
kingdom.*

*But now Mr. Great-Heart replied, "I am a servant of the God of
Heaven; my business is to persuade sinners to repentance. I am
commanded to do my endeavours to turn men, women and children
'from darkness to light, and from the power of Satan unto God'; and if
this be indeed the ground of our quarrel let us fall to it as soon as thou
wilt. Then the Giant came up and Mr. Greatheart went to meet him;
and as he went, Greatheart drew his sword.*

CHAPTER SIX

"Other Little Ships"

There is an interesting incident in Mark's Gospel where we read that as well as the boats of Peter and Andrew and James and John there were "other little ships" that made up the flotilla of vessels on the Sea of Galilee. They may have been smaller than the 'flagship' of the fishing fleet in which Jesus sailed but they get honourable mention here (Mark 4.36) and we may be sure were equally important in Jesus's eyes.

By analogy we would dare to suggest that while T. S. Mooney was ever and always a Churchman, he nevertheless had a warm heart and a deep concern about the "other little ships" that sail in the wake of what we call 'organised religion'. Indeed in T.S.'s view of the Church — and it comes from the New Testament — they also are part of the "Grand Fleet" of Christ. "Ubi Christus, ibi Eccelsia"! (Where Christ is, there is the Church.) That is what T.S. believed and so must we. In any case, that is why he threw in his lot with such organisations as the Bible Society, the Qua Iboe Mission, the Londonderry Christian Workers' Union, the Portstewart Convention, the Faith Mission, the Temperance Movement and others beside. He was selective, of course, and so are we all. There are limits to what we can do with our time and our energy, and he wanted to use both well for the sake of the Captain of his salvation.

The Londonderry Christian Workers' Union

The Londonderry Christian Workers' Union was one of many that came together in the 1920s following the W. P. Nicholson missions throughout Ulster. Those who had been converted at that time came from different Christian Churches but they wanted to continue, to some extent, at least, the cross-denominational meetings for prayer and evangelism. They wished to maintain in their area the strong evangelistic concern and thrust to which they had become accustomed. They had no intention of withdrawing their zeal and prayers from the work of their own places of worship but they wished to give expression to it in an interdenominational way as well. There were risks in this perhaps but the Londonderry C.W.U. was led by wise and

41

earnest men from the local churches who made it a source of evangelistic power and light, in the city and for miles around.

Mr. Joseph Goligher was the owner of Stevenson's Bakery in William Street in the city and shortly after Mr. Mooney arrived in Derry, Mr. Goligher called at the Bank and invited him to take a share in this work. It was a simple thing that he did but a great deal came out of it. It led to a lasting friendship between the two men, however dissimilar in age at the time, and it led to T.S.'s association with the C.W.U. in Londonderry, an interest which was still unbroken at the time of his death. What was it that drew T. S. Mooney to the C.W.U.? For one thing he was attracted because he loved to hear the Gospel preached simply, and clearly and well. Some preachers think that they have become too learned and they fail to do the first. Others become so concerned about technique and other matters as to fail to do the second, and of course, they all fail to do the third. A former Moderator of the Presbyterian Church in England, W. Purves Boyd once said, "Wherever there is preaching it should be central, basic and vital". That's saying the same thing.

T.S. therefore loved to hear the Gospel preached plainly. He would sometimes talk around the fireside of those tendencies of the sinful heart of man to turn God's simple plan of salvation into a difficult, confused and disappointing effort to gain salvation by its own effort instead of taking it by simple faith.

The poet, Cowper's words were much to his liking:
> Oh, how unlike the complex works of man
> Heaven's easy artless, unencumbered plan;
> No meretricious graces to beguile,
> No clustering commands to clog the pile,
>
> ....
>
> Legible only by the light they give
> Stand the soul-quickening words, Believe and Live.
> Too many, shocked at what should charm them most
> Despise the plain direction and are lost.
> "Heaven on such terms"! they cry with proud disdain,
> Incredible, impossible and vain"
> Rebel because 'tis easy to obey
> And scorn for its own sake the gracious way.

So T.S. would say to every Gospel preacher, "Don't make it easy, but by every means make it plain."

This is not to suggest that T.S. ever over-simplified the Gospel and made it a diluted "Come-to-Jesus" affair. The Gospel as he understood it was a far, far bigger thing than that. One could even use the words that Prof. J. S. Stewart used to describe Rev. Alexander Frazer of Tain to describe T.S. as well. He stood for "the breadth and sweep of the essential Gospel. By it he lived and all his days were lyrical in its joy and fruitful in its power."

Then, in the C.W.U. he loved the opportunity to preach the Gospel. There were several mission halls in the city and in the country around that welcomed him gladly. If he did not go himself he was delighted to introduce some of the Magee College students and perhaps even share the service with them. The Londonderry City Mission was one of these and two others in the country were at Curryfree and Lismacarroll. T.S. used to talk of 'the luxury of preaching the Gospel', not that he considered it something to be used sparingly and only on special occasions, but that to engage in it was a privilege and an honour.

One particular part of the preacher's art he excelled at was in telling the seekers, young and old, just how to take that first step 'into Christ'. That gallant Methodist, W. E. Sangster, used to say that the most neglected word in preaching is "HOW". It may be true of many but it certainly was not so with T.S. Who that ever heard him will forget how he explained 'faith' as a five-fingered exercise, *Forsaking All I Take Him*, and then he backed it up by quoting that magnificent answer in the Shorter Cathechism, "Faith in Jesus Christ is a saving grace whereby we receive and rest upon Christ alone for salvation as He is offered in the Gospel."

He did not use flowery words, certainly not in his summing-up or in his final appeal. He simply told them "HOW".

Above all, he was not ashamed of the Gospel as popular speakers are sometimes tempted to be. He knew that there is an offence about the Cross but he was prepared in this respect to bear the shame and obloquy of being a follower of a crucified Saviour, and to endure hardness as a good soldier of the Young Prince of glory Who died for him. We might well sum up this description of T.S.'s Gospel preaching by quoting from Ian Maclaren (Rev. Dr. John Watson) at his first service in Sefton Park Church, Liverpool, "I will not try to astound you with any display of learning, nor attract you by mere eloquence of words, but I promise, by the grace of God and according to my ability, to preach the Cross of Christ." T.S. often quoted that himself. To him this was the preacher's passport; he dare not preach without it. T.S. was of the same conviction and in the same fine company.

All we have said above must not suggest that he used the C.W.U. to boost his own ego and enhance his own reputation. Nothing could be further from the truth. His loyalty to the Union was outstanding, both before 1950 when there were great crowds at the Guildhall services, and after it when they began to decline because many Protestants moved across the river to the Waterside. The new crop of riots in 1968 accelerated this movement and in December 1975 the Sunday services in the Guildhall ceased altogether.

T.S. never ceased to be optimistic about the future of the C.W.U. in Derry. He often expressed his faith that the troubles would cease and the people come back to live on the city side; also that the Sunday Gospel services would be restarted and revived as of old. His optimism was not shared by many, but T.S. was no "quitter" and he felt strongly that the small Fellowship meetings on Friday evenings should continue until peace and revival came.

His usefulness to the C.W.U. can scarcely be put into words. He was a frequent speaker and a versatile one at that. The members often said that while most preachers are gifted as either Gospel preachers, or speakers to Christians, or as Bible teachers, he was gifted in all these ways. The small Londonderry C.W.U. has now lost all this, and in addition is without his energetic leadership, his wise counsel and his cheerful encouragement . . . It has, of course proud and grateful memories, but it also knows that "a great man and a prince has this day fallen in Israel."

J.T.C.

Compiled from tributes paid to T.S. by Mr. R. A. Rankin and Mr. Wm. McCloskey in the Londonderry C.W.U.

The Qua Iboe Mission

It was a Russian Orthodox leader who startled a largely Western audience by saying, "Atheists have a right to be ambiguous, but not Christians." That is like something T. S. Mooney would have said about the missionary obligation of

44

Christian people. Jesus said, "Go ye into all the world" and T.S. believed that He meant just that. In a day of theological ambiguity when there is much talk of consensus and synthesis with world religions it was refreshing to meet a simple down-to-earth man who was resoundingly dogmatic because he was, he believed, honestly Christian. "I am THE Way . . . no man cometh unto the Father but by ME", "Neither is there salvation in any other. There is NONE OTHER NAME", T.S. saw no reason for giving any meaning other than the obvious one to these words. He believed that the Christian Church was born with a map of the world in its hand and it can never close its ears to the Master's "GO."

So he threw his whole weight behind the missionary appeal in his own church, not only overseas, but Continental, and Jewish as well. For the same reason he was a strong supporter of the Qua Iboe Mission (now being better known as the Qua Iboe Fellowship), that Ulster-born and Ulster-based Society on which the blessing of God has rested throughout the 99 years of its work in Nigeria. Once again, after loyal service to the local Auxiliary of the Mission in Londonderry he was invited to join the Council in 1948 and the minutes will bear record that no member of Council was more faithful in attendance than he was. The Qua Iboe Council will never know how many other committees, if they wanted T.S. to attend had to have their meeting either the day before or after because T.S. had to be up in Belfast in the interests of Qua Iboe.

It was one of the greatest trips of his lifetime when he visited the churches of the Qua Iboe Fellowship in 1954 and surely there never was a more gracious and encouraging delegate from the home supporters to bring greetings to the local Christians there. It is a thousand pities that he kept no detailed diary and left no personal report of that visit. It was looked upon as a significant event by the missionaries and as an unforgettable pleasure by himself.

One other side of his missionary interest we know only dimly but with great admiration and even envy, namely, the faithfulness of his prayers for the missionaries themselves. He never spoke about this but those at the receiving end knew a little of it and miss it now that he is no longer with us.

J.T.C.

45

The Bible Society

Mr. Jim McDonald, M.B.E. was in a good position to know what T.S. meant to the great Bible Society and its world-wide responsibility for Bible distribution:

"When I was appointed Northern Ireland secretary for the Bible Society in 1942 he had been treasurer of the Londonderry Auxiliary for some time. He held this office till 1976 when he became the Auxiliary's Chairman.

"His consistent Christian witness gave us a good name all through the North-West and his business training and expertise contributed not a little to the good standing of the Bible Society in all the Churches and to the success which rewarded the efforts of representatives and collectors in the various Christian communions.

"His own love for the Bible was, of course, infectious. It could have been said of him that, 'He learned it, he loved it and he lived it.' It was natural that he should bend his energies to the task of making it possible that all men should have the Scriptures in their own language at a price they could afford. To this enthusiasm for Bible distribution he added a superbly balanced judgement and a trained business acumen, and they all played an important part in widening and deepening the local interest in this work that was so dear to his heart."

The Portstewart Convention

These great gatherings in the delightful surroundings of this beautiful seaside town have had an immense influence on innumerable lives and this has been felt in every part of Ireland and to the ends of the earth as well. T.S. rejoiced to see the grace of God in it and for over fifty years was a regular attender. Indeed long before he became a member of the Convention committee he motored down daily from Londonderry and back again in the evening; or he would arrange to stay the entire week and motor up in the morning to be in his office, and he was meticulous about being in good time.

There were few other people who could have competed with him in recalling the speakers and addresses of the "yester years".

Indeed he had a quite remarkable remembrance of the content of addresses given by this speaker or that, so that when he accepted an invitation to join the committee he brought with him a considerable knowledge and experience of the message and meaning of the Keswick movement.

While he was so well aware of the specific purpose for which the Convention came into being, i.e. the deepening of the spiritual life of Christian people, an important aspect of that week in Portstewart for T.S. was the opportunity it gave him to introduce young ministers and other students to the Convention speakers. These speakers were usually men widely experienced in pulpit and pastoral ministry and he wanted the younger men, especially the divinity men, to meet them and know them. So he organised informal gatherings specially for them when some relevant theological issues were propounded and discussed, and where contemporary moral problems were also given an airing. T.S. was in his element in these off-shoot gatherings and there is not a doubt but that many a man was strengthened in the Faith and the more established in Biblical theology and experimental holiness. Not least, many of them realised that if they were to hold fast the faithful Word, and preach and defend the Gospel of God, it would be of little worth if they did not do both with the anointing grace and power of the Holy Spirit.

It is a known fact that the speakers themselves were often impressed by T.S. and they commented on his well-developed mind, his clarity of thought, his grasp of Reformed theology as well as his aptness of phrase in expressing his own point of view, whatever the subject under discussion. In my correspondence as secretary of the Convention former speakers enquired continually about him and wished to be remembered to him. Even as I write I can recall this being the case with speakers who had come from England, Scotland, Wales, Canada, U.S.A., Australia and New Zealand. There was surely something special about this man and the most beautiful thing of all was that he was the one least conscious of any such thing.

He was the obvious choice of the Committee to succeed Mr. G. M. Walker as honorary treasurer in 1966. In this capacity he was to serve for 19 years, being widely known and respected by all the Convention's friends. His presentation of the financial accounts at the Thursday morning meeting of the Convention each year was a unique occasion; there was no other just like it. He presented the facts and figures, and he enlivened the proceedings with his pawky humour and pungent comment. Whether the audience remembered the figures he gave them was another matter entirely, but they went away knowing that the financial affairs of the convention were in trustworthy hands.

All that I have written and known of T. S. Mooney goes to make up a man of indomitable spirit who never spared himself and was untiring in his work for the Kingdom of God. In 1976 he underwent heart surgery at the hands of the late Mr. Philip Caves, F.R.C.S. who was one of his former Crusader Camp boys and who himself acknowledged his indebtedness under God to T.S. Philip had been appointed in charge of the whole cardiac surgery programme in Scotland before the hand of death took him from us in the midst of a career of great usefulness. With amazing resilience T.S. recovered from his operation and was back in harness with a surprisingly heavy round of commitments which he fulfilled with regularity and faithfulness. Wordsworth in his "Happy Warrior" depicted him to a nicety:

> "Who comprehends his trust, and to the same
> Keeps faithful with a singleness of aim;
> ....
> And while the mortal mist is gathering, draws
> His breath in confidence of Heaven's applause."

The saintly Dr. Alexander Smellie, who was not only one of the early speakers at Portstewart Convention but was also brother-in-law of T.S.'s boyhood minister at Dromore Original Secession Church, used to say, "It is possible for a man to hearken so habitually to conscience, to watch so sedulously God's ways in Providence, and to dwell so much in the company of the divine Word, that scarcely ever will his judgment lead him astray." That is fair comment to make on T. S. Mooney and it is an honest one.

One further thing I, at least, want to say and with the greatest of emphasis. It is that the untiring service which T. S. Mooney rendered was to God, to God Himself. The organisations through which the service was channelled were incidental. The glory of God and the extension of His Kingdom was the goal toward which he strove. To His God, Who is also ours, we give thanks upon every remembrance of His servant.

James McDonald

The young banker!
(c.1930).

CHAPTER SEVEN

T.S.: The Man

The great Dr. Samuel Johnson said that a man should keep his friendships in constant repair. A greater and a wiser said it even better, "A man who has friends must show himself friendly."

T.S. kept both commandments, not through design but through desire. When he gave his heart to Christ in days of youth he found and never lost the Saviour's love for others. I have heard him quoting from John Masefield's "Everlasting Mercy" and two lines in the poem well describe the result of his own conversion

"I knew that Christ had given me birth
To brother all the souls on earth . . ."

When we think of T.S.'s commitment to the work of the Kingdom in Ireland and over the world, the young men he led to Christ, the friends he made and kept, we can say that, in an even wider way than Masefield meant, he made full proof of his ministry.

So much so that a chapter like this on T.S.'s quality of friendship could have been written by any one of thousands of people. Because it isn't written by every one of them, there are thousands of things left out.

I met T.S. first when I went to Magee College in 1945. Some of us were wandering about Woolworth's when he bore down on us, umbrella at the ready, demanded introductions all round and invited us to the Crusaders' Class on Sunday and to tea afterwards at 9 Clarence Avenue.

From the 1930's on, this was a familiar enough pattern for many students at Magee. During the War young men in the Services swelled the numbers and taxed the resources of the Misses Pollock's tea-table on Sunday afternoons.

But T.S. had a legitimate pattern of cross-border shopping that allowed the two ladies to cook and bake and serve with an almost prodigal abandon. And anyone who knew them would have to add — with a pleasure equal to his own.

51

I had always read in the best boys' stories of tables groaning with food, but T.S.'s Sunday tea-table turned fiction into fact, though it is only in restrospect I realise the labour of love that was involved in producing such a happy effect.

Yet tea-time was only an interlude. There was the obvious welcome, the fire in the upstairs drawing-room that was more than a match for the winter winds, and the surprising knowledge of young men's hearts and hopes that made conversation flow and the shyest student feel instantly at home.

Reader, remember that this is not a description of an isolated Sunday afternoon. It was T.S.'s constant practice and anyone who ever enjoyed it would be quick to say that it was far from being a formality. He gave himself for his guests and he obviously enjoyed every moment of the conversation and the crack.

This may seem the more remarkable when we place the weekly tea parties in the middle of a Sabbath well-spent. T.S. had already taken a morning Bible Class before the Great James' Street service. In the afternoon he had spoken to his Crusaders and would be going on to the evening service. After that there was the C.W.U. meeting in the Guildhall and possibly a sick call or a supper engagement before the day was done.

T.S. was the Master's man for others and all these activities were the things that made the Sabbath a delight and his well-filled day his reasonable service.

It is no trite abuse of language to say that only eternity will reveal how much the Presbyterian Church owed and owes to an all-wise Divine strategy that placed such an evangelical layman with unusual qualities of wisdom, wit and warmth, in the very city where students for the ministry were trained.

There is certainly no chance relationship between T. S. Mooney's influence and the rise and usefulness of the Evangelical Union in Magee College. He supported its witness to students, served on its advisory committee and spoke when asked at its meetings. His unswerving purpose was to lift many a Divinity student's sights to the ideal of the man of God, throughly furnished unto all good works.

T.S.'s favourite Bible Studies with students were in Paul's letters to Timothy. Many of us profited from the broad sweep of his dissertation on Timothy's Walk, Work and Warfare and still benefit from his asides — "No man is as good as he might be, unless he is as fit as he can be,"or on Timothy's personal commitment to Christ apart from his Christian background, — "A man is always better in Christian work after he has been converted."

T.S.'s admitted excellence as an expositor is easily traced to his life-long study of the Word. As well as knowing his Bible he was widely read in Christian commentary, the history of the Church was a source book for edification and there were few who confronted his theology and came away unscathed.

As a first year student, after some slight toe-dipping in reformed teaching, I ventured to suggest to him, by way of clinching a discussion on the Lord's Supper, that Zwingli was not far from the truth. I was sure he would be glad to change the subject. I knew little of Zwingli and less of T.S.

"I grant you," T.S. said, "that Zwingli had much to commend him . . ." I found out in the years since that this was an opening move, typical of T.S. and equivalent to forfeiting a man at draughts and going on to lift a line of kings. And so indeed he proceeded with Zwingli's distinctive position as compared to Luther and Calvin, going on to weigh all three in the scales of Scripture truth and, without a trace of condescension, leaving me to draw my own conclusions.

Here it may be said that in all kinds of debate and in the ordinary intimacies of fireside conversation, T.S.'s great strengths were his gifts of recollection and recall. Names, events, dates, broad considerations and meticulous details came forward when required, easily accessible from the shelves of a well-stocked, well-ordered mind.

Yet not many people lived a fuller or busier life, with less time for study. His business in the Bank required good timekeeping, but not for T.S. the arrival just in time that satisfies most of us. For many years he was the first to arrive to sort the mail and set things in order so that there was no delay when the staff came in. He never required the injunction at Assembly's College to "guard well your morning hours."

George Johnstone Jeffrey, in his lectures on preaching, twice quotes what he called his favourite text, Job 38:12, "Hast thou commanded the morning?" T.S., who was not his own master once the working day began, commanded the morning long before he let himself into the Bank. Even on holiday his Bible and his books for study were by his bed and, right up until recent times, when staying with us, we would have heard him moving from six o'clock on.

In his banking days, he would have got up anywhere, at any hour, to make sure that he arrived back in Londonderry's Shipquay Street, to be in the office by half past eight.

My student assistantship was spent with Rev. James Dunlop in Oldpark Church. No chapter on T.S. and friendship could leave out the brotherly relationship between these two. T.S. and James Dunlop were friends from what are now being called by older people "the early days." In their case it was more precisely described by the latter when he said that his friendship with T.S. went back to the time when, both newly converted, they conducted open-air meetings together in North Antrim, T.S. with his Coleraine Inst. cap and James Dunlop wearing his from Ballymena Academy.

Other chapters will indicate the common interests in the Lord's work that they shared together for a lifetime.

For many years T.S. motored to Belfast for evening meetings, staying at the Oldpark Manse and returning in the early hours of the morning. Sometimes he had to be started off with a push from the minister and his wife, aided by shipyardmen on their way to catch the first tram, but I never heard of an occasion when he didn't make it.

His notification of these visits was usually by telephone to the lady of the Manse and followed a set pattern, surprising in a man who shunned fixed forms in other fields. "This is the Bishop of Derry speaking. Is the prophet's chamber available for tomorrow evening?"

These overnight trips were much sought after by students looking for a lift to Belfast and T.S. was well-known to prefer company other than his own. They were always journeys worth remembering, and not only for the quality of the conversation. His black Sunbeam-Talbot was low-slung on the road and therefore its centre of gravity lower still. This was a happy design used by the Creator to preserve His servant without recourse to actual intervention in the laws of the universe.

In those days of petrol rationing every motorist had his own favourite means of saving fuel. T.S.'s was more hair-raising than most. He switched off the engine and went into neutral at the top of the Glenshane Pass.

It was a deeply religious experience to watch the speedometer needle pass 80 and have nowhere else to go, whilst the driver continued his dissertation with an occasional resort to the use of fist and palm for emphasis. The road then was a narrow switchback, though mercifully free of oncoming traffic and certainly with nothing passing. The sound of the engine coming on again when gravity caught up with us was sweeter than a heavenly choir and, for a few miles, even less expected.

When I was called to Kilkeel in 1955 I had high hopes of returning a little of T.S.'s abundant hospitality. His well-filled weekends, however, made this something of a problem — and a lesson in faithfulness as well to a young minister sorting out priorities in his first charge.

The only Sunday the Crusader Class didn't meet was Whit, therefore that was the only weekend T.S. allowed himself to be free.

So that became the arrangement and from then until he retired he came to us every Whit, whatever other times he might call, in between.

In process of time the Crusader Easter House Party came to Mourne Grange School at Kilkeel and T.S. was glad to succumb to the temptation of a bed in one or other of the Manses. By this time he was easing himself out of many of his responsibilities and — best tribute to his leadership — other younger men were readily available to carry on his work.

These Easter House Parties moved to Newcastle coincidentally with my own call in 1970. T.S. was now retired from the Bank and enjoyed much freedom of choice in his acceptance of invitations. His annual visits to us were transferred to Easter so that he could still associate with the Crusaders.

It was interesting as it was instructive to see that he was as acceptable to the boys as when he was in charge and, history repeating itself, always in demand to ferry a car load of boys to Newcastle or take them home again.

But by 1975, T.S. was visibly slowing up. The disabilities and the inabilities of a tired heart were multiplying despite his valiant efforts to maintain his interests and commitments. Privately, he admitted his frustration and confessed that he was finding it hard to live with his limitations.

Help, however, was at hand. In the following year Philip Caves, keen Christian, one of T.S.'s boys, and a Crusader leader and brilliant surgeon at Glasgow Royal Infirmary, prevailed on T.S. to go there for examination and eventual surgery.

It was a great success. I went over to visit him a couple of days after the operation. His sister and a friend were at his bedside. His pleasure at the visit was obvious. I was flattered until he told me I had been sent to do something he could not do for himself. It was to take the ladies out for tea. This was more important than the operation and its result. He was emphatic that it was his treat and he must pay.

There was no arguing with him, or rather the argument ended when the ward sister advanced to put us out for upsetting her patient. We left with as much of T.S.'s money as would have bought the table and the tea service as well as the tea. His voice, though fainter than usual followed us down the ward. "Now, brother, this is why you were sent to see me."

It was almost two years after this, when he was with us again at Newcastle, that a phone call came from his friend John T. Carson. Philip Caves, the Christian surgeon with the brilliant mind and skilful hands had died suddenly during a game of squash, the victim of a massive coronary thrombosis.

Could we break the news gently to T.S., preferably when he was sitting down in the afternoon? Lunch was difficult, for T.S. had no reason to be other than cheerful whilst we had every reason to be apprehensive.

Afterwards, with T.S. carefully seated at the fire, we told him the sad news; Philip Caves called home so tragically, it seemed, at the height of his career and at only 39 years of age.

T.S. was much moved. He shook his head as if to bring himself out of a bad dream. Then he stood up unsteadily. We were a little circle of three. "He saved my life," he said, "And yet he couldn't save his own."

Somehow, suddenly, we were back at Calvary.

56

That was a moment when such a reflection was very understandable. But those who kept company with T. S. Mooney will not need to be told how often a seemingly ordinary conversation would take on deeper dimensions, the servant speaking naturally of his Master's work. Indeed it was impossible for T.S. to talk long on any subject without beginning to communicate the sweet fragrance of knowing Him.

Those two great preachers, Alexander Whyte and Marcus Dods, had the habit of going for long walks on Saturday afternoons. Describing their conversation, Whyte used to say, "Whatever we started off with, we soon made across country to Jesus of Nazareth."

T.S. would have been wholly at home in their company. In groups as small as two or three, or gatherings as large as the General Assembly, he never aimed to draw attention to himself, but was always eager to talk about his Lord.

It has often been said that T.S. had the happy knack of keeping friendships in repair. But this was no mere unconscious facility. No one appreciated more the fellowship of kindred minds and no one had better manners in acknowledging the debt that friendship owes to foresight.

Wherever he had been entertained or obliged, a letter of thanks arrived within days, or an immediate phone call to express his appreciation.

Indeed, his correspondence followed his friends across the world. Not for him the cold formality of a typewritten note. His pen was the tongue of the ready writer and his letters were legion. After his death, quite unexpectedly, a missionary's wife said to me, "T.S. wrote to us regularly, without fail, all the years we were abroad." There must have been many, far from home, in lonely situations, who gave thanks for the sight of the Londonderry postmark and the distinctive carefree, careful writing on the envelope.

Unlike most of us, T.S. did not find with the passing of the years that interests fail and friends grow few. He maintained his interests and he renewed his friendships. These were, more often than not, with younger men in the ministry, the Crusader movement and the evangelical societies, missionary and evangelistic, where he found himself so much at home.

And he had other friendships, equally cherished over the years and nourished from other affinities. One that he valued more than most was with Professor R. L. Marshall of Magee College, though for many years the two were unacquainted.

Sometimes I was asked to speak at the Sunday evening C.W.U. meeting in the Guildhall. This included the pleasure of a weekend with T.S. or Mr. Joe Goligher and before leaving, a visit to Dr. Marshall, who was inclined to be cross if he were omitted. It was on one of these occasions T.S. remarked that he had never met R. L. Marshall, adding that he had always liked the sound of him!

I rang Mrs. Marshall to say that I was bringing along an admirer of her husband and his work. The two men were in instant accord. This was the beginning of a close and valued friendship on both sides which lasted until Professor Marshall's death. Despite my limited introduction, T.S., whose standards in ministers' wives were exacting in the extreme, had the highest opinion of Mrs. Marshall also and continued to visit her until she too passed away.

Apart from every other friendship he formed, T.S.'s interest in boys, for themselves and for their Saviour, leaves a record of Christian concern unequalled here in Ireland and, in its abiding influence, possibly surpasses all his other work.

A caring and compassionate insight into young men's minds through recollection of his own, added immeasurably to his ability to communicate the Gospel. T.S. had a downright way of speaking that was entirely characteristic of his personality. He spoke to them without condescension and without cant. He talked to them from the platform in the same natural voice he used when he was driving them out of the Strand sweetshop on a Sunday, chiding them back to bed at a Crusader House party, or discussing themselves, their school, their family, their ambitions.

The Gospel according to T. S. Mooney was as factual, as real an issue, as demanding of an answer as any other part of life.

It was often told of W. G. Ovens, another man for boys, that, when he was asked to put his name in autograph books at C.S.S.M. gatherings, he often wrote the same verse. The words are as applicable to T.S. as ever they were to that great saint of Scripture Union.

"My album is the schoolboy's breast
Where evil powers seek to wrest
And win a bright young life.

To write the Name of Jesus there,
And point to worlds more bright and fair,
And see the schoolboy kneel in prayer,
Is my supreme delight."

Now that his work on earth is ended, it is possible to look back along the length of his life and read the reason for his usefulness; so simple, so sublime and, unfortunately, so rare; Chaucer saw it long ago in another unassuming and consistent Christian . . .

Christ's lore and His Apostles twelve
He taught, but first
He followed it himselve."

Smiley Fullerton

MOONEYISMS

The name of T. S. Mooney will never get you into Heaven; but could gain you an entrance into most Christian gatherings on earth.

As Treasurer of several organisations T.S. often used his fund of humour to bait the hook he was throwing out in the hope of larger donations. Referring to an American book on giving with the title, "A Tip or a Tithe", T.S. was heard to say, "Too often the offerings in our churches come under the first of these descriptions."

Sometimes he baited the hook so well with a humorous story that the audience failed to snap at it because they were laughing so heartily all the time. He compared himself to a highwayman holding them up and saying, "Your money or your life." He did not fail to let his hearers know that they were like an Irishman who, when threatened in that way, said, "You can take my life for I need my money."

T.S. with the "Frazers of Tain."

CHAPTER EIGHT

The Scottish Connection

It was as a young Probationer fulfilling my Assistantship in Springburnhill, Glasgow with Dr. William Fitch, in the early post-war years — 1948 to be precise — that I first met T. S. Mooney. This was the beginning of a friendship which was to span nearly four decades, and which led latterly over the past considerable number of years to the inclusion of our Manse as one of his 'ports of call' during his annual Scottish 'pilgrimage'. It was only gradually, however, that the realisation came of how much this warm-hearted, lovable Ulsterman knew about the Scottish scene, and how thirled he was to what is best in the spiritual life of the Scottish Church.

He had, of course, a genius for friendship, and this does much to explain why he needed to be 'across the water' regularly to maintain contact with so many of us, and with the steady stream of young folk from Ulster — students, Crusaders and others — whom he referred to our congregations for fellowship and pastoral care. And not a passing contact either, but something in depth, with a shrewd and penetrating assessment of movements and currents in the ecclesiastical and theological scene in our land. His finger was 'on the pulse' so to speak of Scottish Church life, and he had the advantage of being able to assess it from an outside perspective as a member of a sister Church. His shrewd theological perception, his connection with and participation in Scottish IVF (UCCF), his long acquaintance with Scottish Church history and personalities, in Church of Scotland and Free Church alike — few laymen I have known have been better or more deeply read — all these combined to make him a man of judgment and discernment, and one to be listened to with profound respect. It was our privilege and pleasure to welcome him to the gatherings of evangelical ministers in Scotland and to share fellowship with him in matters that were of common concern in the life of our churches.

Two experiences may be mentioned at this point as standing out for me in my association with T.S. One is the unfailing

61

regularity with which, when he stayed in our home, he seemed to find it necessary to make contact, either by telephone or by personal meeting, with students and other Ulster exiles, some now ministers and some business men, who had passed through his hands in former years. He had an impressive, even extraordinary, circle of people whom he had in his prayers, and this extended to Scotsmen also, with whom over many years he had had association and fellowship in the interests of the kingdom of God. His Scottish pilgrimages were never times of rest and relaxation, but invariably purposeful and fruitful in deepening Christian fellowship.

The other is the fact that T.S. was instrumental in introducing me, principally through the Portstewart Convention, to a great company of Ulster evangelicals, and this is assuredly a rich and enriching debt I owe to him, and for which I shall always be grateful to God. One memory in particular will remain of a visit to the Convention to which, at T.S.'s invitation, I travelled across a day or two early, and was given right royal hospitality, with a visit to Alan and Anne Flavelle's lovely manse in Kilkeel, and a tour around Co. Donegal, savouring its quiet beauties. It was an idyllic introduction to the week of ministry at Portstewart.

There are not all that many men of whom it can be said, as John Buchan said of one of his greatest friends, that "his presence warmed and lit up so big a region of life that in thinking of him one is overwhelmed by the multitude of things that he made better by simply existing among them." But many would want to say something like this of T. S. Mooney. It is not so much that he was 'larger than life' — although you would not be so far off the mark to use such a phrase of him — as that he was utterly real. The warmth and humanity of the man was impressive, and the power this had to draw friendship and affection, as well as immense respect and esteem, can be seen in the wealth of the numbers who were glad and counted themselves privileged to call him their friend. And withal, the irrespressible humour, in which that warm humanity was so often expressed and displayed! T.S. would have loved what G. F. Bradby once wrote to William Temple on the occasion of his approaching marriage: "I am glad you are going to marry. I am always glad when anybody marries: for though it diminishes the number of the elect, it adds to the number of reasonable human beings." Bachelor though he was, and notably one of the elect, T.S. was one of the most reasonable human beings known to any of us.

What James Denney, one of his favourite Scottish authors, says of St. Paul could with a considerable measure of truth, *nutatis mutandis*, be said also of him. Speaking of the loneliness of the apostolic vocation, in which he had given up everything for Christ's sake, Denney refers to our Lord's words in Luke 18:29,30 about the rewards of such faithfulness, and adds

"We may be sure that not one of those who were most richly blessed with all these natural relations and natural affections knew better than he what love is. No father ever loved his children more tenderly, fervently, austerely and unchangeably than Paul loved those whom he had begotten in the gospel. No father was ever rewarded with affection more genuine, obedience more loyal, than many of his converts rendered to him. Even in the trials of love, which search it, and strain it, and bring out its virtues to perfection — in misunderstandings, ingratitude, wilfulness, suspicion — he had an experience with blessings of its own in which he surpassed them all. If love is the true wealth and blessedness of our life, surely none was richer or more blessed than this man."

T.S. was surely given the hundredfold in this life, brothers and sisters and mothers and children: he was rich in the truest and best sense of the word.

How may we best describe the influence of this gracious man of God in terms that will be intelligible and persuasive to those who have known him? Well, in a day when many winds of change have been blowing across the face of our fractured society, and many currents have been flowing in the the social and religious life of our time, it is impressive to realise that few people, if any — and certainly not this writer — will be able to recall a time when T.S. was ever different from the man we had always known him to be. You always knew where this man stood, and what he stood for. Here was constancy, and rock-like consistency and stability, that could always be depended upon to be there, an unchanging point of reference from which it was possible to take one's bearings in any situation of uncertainty or confusion.

It is this rock-like quality that brings to mind a wonderfully impressive and evocative exposition of Isaiiah 32:2 by George Adam Smith, one of the greatest of Old Testament scholars, another Scotsman with whose writings T.S. was familiar:

> "A man shall be as a hiding place from the wind . . .
> as the shadow of a great rock in a weary land".

Pointing out that while these words find their truest fulfilment in our Lord, Smith insists that through Him their fulfilment can become true of those who follow in His steps. In an extended excursus, full of memorable utterances and 'quotable quotes', he maintains that what the prophet is asking for is for great characters, big men. In a remarkable metaphor describing desert sand in a continual state of drift, bringing a barrenness by which life is stunted or choked, he adds:

> "But set down a rock on the sand, and see the difference its presence makes. After a few showers, to the leeward side of this some blades will spring up; if you have patience, you will see in time a garden. How has the boulder produced this? simply by arresting the drift."

> "Now that is exactly how great men benefit human life. A great man serves his generation, serves the whole race, by arresting the drift . . . History is swept by drifts: superstition, error, poisonous custom, dust-laden controversy. What has saved humanity has been the upraising of some great man to resist those drifts, to set his will, strong through faith, against the prevailing tendency, and be the shelter of the weaker, but not less desirous, souls of his brethren."

Great men, says Smith, "are not the whole of life, but they are the condition of all the rest; if it were not for the big men, the little ones could scarcely live. The first requisites of religion and civilisation are outstanding characters."

Those who knew T.S. will know in what substantial measure these words reflect the rock-like quality of his life, and just how many found in the leeward side of his faith a shelter where the growth of true spiritual life became a possibility for them. And what a gracious and reassuring shelter it was! Smith's stricture on the 'unco-guid' was never remotely true of him: "Some righteous people have a terribly north-eastern exposure; children do not play about their doors, nor the prodigal stop there."

If we may speak of any legacy that he has left, it would surely be that by the inspiration of his life, and its testimony to 'the faith once delivered to the saints', he should have pointed so unambiguously towards the need for men and women of stature and integrity, able to inject moral vision into public life. The following lines, taken from a missionary magazine, whose origin is unknown to the writer, might well have been his prayer:

God give us men. The time demands
Strong minds, great hearts, true faith and willing hand;
Men whom the lust of office does not kill.
Men whom the spoils of office cannot buy;
Men who possess opinions and a will.
Men who have honour; men who will not lie.
Men who can stand before a demagogue
And damn his treacherous flatteries without winking;
Tall men; sun-crowned, who live above the fog
In public duty and in private thinking.

The world will seem a poorer place for his passing, for it has left a bigger hole in the Christian life of Ulster than will be easily filled. As we salute his memory and give thanks for all that he meant to us, we reflect, in the words that John Buchan wrote of his friend, that "it is the kind of loss least easy to forget, and yet one which soon comes to be contemplated without pain, for he had succeeded most fully in life."

MOONEYISM

He used to go over the outline of a sermon on "The Penitent Thief" which he traced to his boyhood minister. At 9 a.m. he was out of Christ. At 12 noon he was in Christ. At 12 midnight he was with Christ. What a crowded and eventful day in one man's life!

GREATHEART

And would you, then, become a Greatheart too?
And would you be employed in your day as
Thomas Smyth Mooney was in his?

*Then expound to yourself and follow out that deep riddle with
which Mr. Greatheart so woke up old Mr. Honest;*

He that will kill, must first be overcome;
Who live abroad would, first must die at home.

*Then do not stop until you discover Mr. Honest's solution of the
riddle;*

He first by grace must conquered be
That sin would mortify;
And who, that lives, would convince me
Unto himself must die.

*for, as a greater than them all said, by His words and by His Cross
"Except a corn of wheat fall into the ground and die, it abideth alone,
but if it die it bringeth forth much fruit."*

*THERE IS NO EASY WAY TO SPIRITUAL INFLUENCE AND
POWER.*

CHAPTER NINE

Going Steadily for the Top

Few finer things have ever been said of those who have risked their lives for an ideal, or in the interests of their fellow men than that which described those two intrepid climbers, Mallory and Irvine, who in 1924 lost their lives in their attempt to conquer Mt. Everest. It was said of them that *"they were last seen going steadily for the top"*. They were nearly there, but they never slackened the pace even at the last stage.

Nothing truer could be said of T. S. Mooney in describing the final years of his life. There was no loss of interest, no fading of early ideals and only a little noticeable slackening of grip and step. Steadily for the top — that was how we last saw him and that is how he will always be remembered. Only four days before he died he was the special guest at a dinner to celebrate the fiftieth anniversary of the Londonderry Young People's Convention — a creation of his own — and some who were present said that he seemed at his most alert and buoyant best. He never lowered his standards. He never slackened his guard against his own weaknesses. He kept his communion with his Lord and Master as green and fresh as if he were a young convert, and if we were trying to find some one single secret of his steadfast endurance it could be found in his simple but faithful communion with his God.

When Sir Winston Churchill died in 1965 Sir Robert Menzies was in London for the funeral. This great Australian Prime Minister and Commonwealth leader broadcast on the B.B.C. a memorable tribute to Sir Winston:

> "With warmth in our hearts and in our recollections many of us will be able to say, "I lived in Churchill's time". Some will be able to say "I knew him. I talked with him. I was his friend."

That historic event involving the greatest political figure of the twentieth century certainly warranted those noble words, but for a host of men and boys, and many more besides, they are just as true and just as worthy of T. S. Mooney. A small army of us are proud to say, "I was in the Londonderry Crusader Class in T. S. Mooney's time." Many more will eagerly claim, "I heard him preach. He was kindness itself to me when I was in difficulties and he helped me over my problem." Yet another legion will confess, "I talked to him face to face when my faith faltered and doubts were near. His words set me on my feet again. I could never forget him." And some more will quietly and gladly say, "He led me to Christ."

I have been trying to analyse what it was in T.S. over the years that makes us grateful to have known him and to have worked alongside of him. There is, first of all, the fact that during the last 50 years which have brought an unprecedented amount of change he stood for what was permanent, and sacred, and eternal.

Of course he belonged to goodly Ulster-Scot stock and that says a lot. It was a former Earl of Rosebery who said, "I love Highlanders, and I love Lowlanders, but when I come back to the branch of our race which has been grafted on to the Ulster stem I take off my hat with veneration and awe." Moreover when the rugged honesty and independence of the Ulster Scot is joined to the courtesy of the native Irish it produces a type of character that is winsome as well as strong. During all these years T.S. stood foursquare to every wind that blew and epitomised for us the things that cannot be shaken with the passage of time.

In addition, and again with no equivocation whatsoever, Tom Mooney stood for the Gospel of God's grace, the old, old story of God's redemption through the precious blood of Christ, and he did it through times when it was often considered something which a man outgrew as he got older and wiser. He, however, kept close to the essentials of the Gospel. He used great simplicity in the words he employed. He never wandered from Christ as the centre of everything and the temptation to be ashamed of the Gospel of a crucified Saviour, so often yielded to by men of learning and supposed good taste, was one he knew well but steadily resisted. There are many people who will always be grateful that he was not ashamed of the Gospel of Christ.

Yet another mark of the consistency of T.S. with which he ran the race and finished the course, was his understanding of young people. He had the wisdom to have patience with and at times to share the soaring ambitions of young men especially. He was sensitive, adaptable, and understanding right to the end, as much as he was through half a century.

There was, of course, a ripeness of character about him which seemed to reduce the ordinary run of men to peasantry. He moved among his fellows with a natural ease and poise, but he was the one who appeared to know nothing about it.

Then, and perhaps the thing that is uppermost in the minds of many in this year of our Lord 1986, is the dogged preserverance and devotion to a task that had been given him by God. Over the years he gave all of his mind, and most of his talents and time to the mission of telling the old, old story, so simply that boys especially should not fail to take it in. This steadfastness "in season, out of season," year after year, was to those of us who looked on, a perpetual inspiration, and to all who worked alongside, an example to be emulated.

What then has all this to say to us ourselves, whether we be youth workers, teachers or preachers, elders or ministers alike? Quite simply and frankly this — that to achieve a life like this and to accomplish a work so enduring, demands great self-discipline, hard mental toil, and utter self-giving. We are all sacredly different and have got to respond to the challenge of this good, wholesome and useful life in our own way.

Let me put it in four terse propositions: each of which and all of which provided the motivation in T.S.'s case.

1. If the Gospel is a matter of life and death, it is surely to be taken seriously. Time and opportunity are not to be trifled with. The Christian life is no mere pastime.

2. If Christ is worth serving at all, He is worth serving well. This was a favourite theme of T.S. Christians are not their own; they are bought with a price. T.S. would often repeat in this connection

   I would not work my soul to save
   For that my Lord has done;
   But I would work like any slave
   For love of God's dear Son.

3. If Jesus wanted his disciples to be fishers of men, who gave any of us the right to be satisfied with providing the tackle and pointing others to the fishing grounds instead of going

ourselves and casting our net until it is filled, or to cast our simple line to win our friends, one by one, for Christ.

4. If I wish to be approved at the last, then let me remember that no intellectual superiority, no eloquence in preaching, no absorption in business, no shrinking temperament, and no spirit of timidity can take the place of or be an excuse for my not making an honest, sincere and prayerful effort to bring others to the Saviour.*

John T. Carson

* These two last paragraphs owe a lot to a page in J. W. Chapman's book, *The Personal Touch*, over which I recall T.S. pondering deeply as he sat at my fireside. They moved him, and they motivated him constantly. J.T.C.

In my life I have received many kindnesses; enough to fill any man's heart with gratitude and to humble his pride in the dust.

The differences in men's view of the Lord's Day is all a matter of a single letter of the alphabet. It is a question of whether Sunday is to be a holy day or a holiday. Let all our folk who seek to make it the latter know assuredly that they are traitors to the Protestant cause.

No excuses can justify our absence from our place in the congregation in church that would not also justify the minister's absence from his place in the pulpit.

Religion is the best armour a person can wear but the worst cloak.

The man who thinks that without mental and spiritual preparation he can hand in a Communion token and sit down as of right at the Lord's Table should read once again the eleventh chapter of First Corinthians and tremble in his shoes.

The WELL-TO-DO do not want the poor to suffer. They wish them to be as happy as is consistent with the continued prosperity of the well-to-do.

GREATHEART

A word from the famous Dr. Alexander Whyte of Edinburgh who seemed to have known and understood Greatheart well.

"Noble Greatheart! Be assured that all this labour is not in vain in thy Lord. Be well assured that not one drop of thy blood, or thy sweat, or thy tears shall fall to the ground on that day when they that be wise shall shine as the brightness of the firmament, and they that turn many to righteousness as the stars for ever and ever."

O Brave Greatheart, put on again thy whole armour. Receive again, and again fulfil, thy Master's commission, till He has no more commissions left for thy brave heart and thy bold hand to execute. And one glorious day, when thou art still returning to thy task, it shall suddenly sound in thy dutiful ears, — "Well done! Good and faithful servant!" And then thou too

"Shalt hang the trumpet in the hall
And study war no more."

Bunyan Characters Vol. 2 pp. 187-188.

CHAPTER TEN

A Very Precious Fragment

"I was converted when I was a girl of 14. An older Christian girl invited me to the Sunday evening service of the Londonderry Christian Workers' Union in the Guildhall. On the first night that I attended, Mr. Mooney was the preacher. As I listened I sat enthralled as he made Christ, and His Cross and His love for me, so real. I have heard him preach many times since that never-to-be-forgotten night and never once has he failed to reach my heart.

After that 'happy day' and ever since I was a teenager Mr. Mooney was always a friend ready to chat before or after a meeting. He had a great love for young people and was right on their wave length. He nevertheless always remained faithful to old-time standards, theological and ethical.

Later when I was married he became a frequent visitor in our house; we both loved him and admired him. From T.S. I learned to love the Church of my adoption. He never failed to put the emphasis here in the right place, He was a Christian first, that was good and essential. To be a Presbyterian in addition, T.S. would say, was better even if not essential.

From time to time he would do a series of Bible Readings on the Friday evenings and I will never forget some of these, especially one on the epistle to the Galatians when he excelled. I will not ever forget what he taught us then about the great doctrine of Justification by Faith alone. How accurately he hit the nail on the head every time.

We will miss him in our home, and in Kilfennan. Even the streets of the city are not the same now that he is gone. I pray that the book of tributes will bring glory to His Saviour for I know that would please him more than anything else."

Anon.

Letters like this are worth more than all the medals and honours that might be conferred on any man. T.S. must have had many such letters and their writers were, to him 'his hope and joy and crown of rejoicing',(1 Thess. 2.19-20). T.S. did not really need any other tribute, for there can be none greater than this.

J.T.C.

GREATHEART

Nearing the end of his Pilgrim journey

"The waters, indeed, are to the palate bitter, and to the stomach, cold; yet the thoughts of what I am going to and of the convoy that wait for me on the other side, lie as a glowing coal at my heart. I see myself now at the end of my journey; my toilsome days are ended. I am going to see that head which was crowned with thorns and that face which was spat upon for me. I have formerly lived by hearsay and faith, but now I go where I shall live by sight and shall be with him in whose company I delight myself. I have loved to hear my Lord spoken of; and wherever I have seen the print of his shoe in the earth, there I have coveted to set my feet too."

GREATHEART

CHAPTER ELEVEN

The Funeral Service of Thanksgiving
in Kilfennan Presbyterian Church, Londonderry

On Friday, 24th January, 1986, we were all saddened to learn of the death of our esteemed Clerk of Session, Mr. Thomas Smyth Mooney ("T.S."). For over sixty years he was a loyal member of Gt. James Street/Kilfennan congregation. He attended his first service in Gt. James Street on the second Sunday in February, 1925. He sat under six ministers and was a prayerful supporter of each one in turn.

The congregation expressed their confidence in him by electing him an elder on 3rd October, 1943, and the Kirk Session unanimously elected him Clerk of Session in September, 1973, following the death of Mr. William Thomson. Throughout his period of service as an elder and Clerk of Session he was thoughtful and efficient, prayerful and faithful. In this capacity he will be very much missed in our congregation.

For many Mr. Mooney will be remembered for his fifty years in the Sunday School (35 of which he was leader of the Bible Class). As one of our present elders said "The catechism only came alive to me when handled so lovingly by T.S."

We gathered with many others on Tuesday afternoon, 28th January, in Kilfennan Presbyterian Church, for a Service of Thanksgiving for the Life and Witness of Mr. Mooney. Over five hundred people met to pay tribute to T.S. and to thank God for his impact on their lives. I had the great honour of leading that service and used the words of 1 Thess. 5 as part of my Call to Worship. The Moderator of the General Assembly, the Right Rev. Robert Dickinson, M.A.,D.D., led the whole congregation in a most meaningful prayer, "after which he expressed the sympathy of the whole General Assembly to us. The Scripture Readings were taken from Psalm 103, Romans 8, John 14 and Philippians 1 v 18-26. The tribute to Mr. Mooney was brought by his great personal friend the Rev. Alan Flavelle, B.A.,D.D. Despite recent ill-health the articulate flair of Dr. Flavelle stimulated all of us to reflect upon the spiritual character of a truly great man. The main prayer of intercession was led by the Very Rev. John T. Carson, B.A.,D.D. Perhaps only he could have kept the balance between sorrow for our loss and the triumph of grace. His words will be remembered for a long time.

The praise was inspiring and Mr. Mooney would have applauded it. Psalm 84 "How lovely is Thy dwelling place", sung to the tune *Harrington* was one of his favourites. So also was the hymn "Lord, in the fulness of my might, I would for Thee be strong." Mr. Mooney's consecration was no fag-end, withered-leaves offering. He brought no sickly sacrifice for God's service. His passion was never a thing of faded fires or burnt-out ashes. The hymn was well chosen and T.S. would have approved the inclusion of that verse, so often omitted in the hymnaries and which he thought one of the best of all because it represented the way he came to Christ Himself.

> I cannot, Lord, too early take
> The covenant divine;
> Oh, ne'er the happy heart shall break
> Whose earliest love was Thine.

The final hymn, *Thine be the glory, Risen, Conquering Son* gave the large congregation a fitting expression of their appreciation to God for T. S. Mooney, their friend.

In the driving snow of Altnagelvin Cemetery we laid all that was mortal of T.S. to rest, thankful, as someone else put it elsewhere, that there was so much that could never be buried or forgotten.

E.S.McK.

The Tribute

May I begin by applying to our friend, "T.S." words that were spoken of W. M. MacGregor by A. J. Gossip? "(T.S.) was a unique personality, so original in the whole make-up of his being that, now that he is gone, something has vanished from us which is entirely irreplaceable;

> "As when a Kingly cedar, green with boughs
> Goes down with a great shout upon the hills,
> And leaves a lonesome place against the sky,"

76

so for those whose lives touched his in his manifold activities, his passing leaves a staring gap which must remain empty and blank."

My first encounter with T.S. was on an evening when he was preaching in First Lurgan Church on the text, "Thou are not far from the kingdom of heaven." Pointing out that the lawyer had come to heckle Jesus, T.S. told of how, in the days of the Suffragettes, Mrs. Pankhurst was making an impassioned plea for women's rights.

Suddenly the spate of her rhetoric subsided, and in the silence that followed, a rather seedy-looking man shouted up: "Don't you wish you were a man?" "No," came the rapier-like reply, "don't you?" The humour and the humanity of the man drew me to him — as it has drawn so many others over the years.

He often said that memories of his earlier years clustered around three buildings: a house, a church and a school.

The house was his home, a farmhouse in North Antrim, where his upbringing was fairly strict. The lasting legacy which he carried away from his home was a love for the Shorter Catechism, which had a formative influence, not only in shaping his thought, but also in shaping the expression of that thought in such a precise way. The Church building was that of the Dromore Original Secession congregation where he sat under the ministry of the Rev. Edward White, who was married to a sister of the well-known author, Alex Smellie. When I asked him what lasting impression Mr. White had left upon him, he said: "From him I learned to love the King's English well-spoken, a Presbyterian service simply conducted and the Gospel of God's grace faithfully preached."

The school-house was at Cullyvenny which, when it ceased to be a school, was leased to two Scotsmen, Faith Mission Pilgrims, for a special Mission. During their visit, T.S. had that conversion experience which marked the beginning of his Christian life. From that point he could make his own words of Paul: "For to me to live is Christ, and to die is gain."

In Christ he found **A PERSON TO FOLLOW.**

For him the essence of the Christian experience was that person-to-person relationship with the Christ who for our sake "died and was raised." He could say with Zinzendorf: "I have only one passion — it is He, only He."

There was A DEEPENING FELLOWSHIP WITH CHRIST. This he cultivated by the study of Scripture and the practice of prayer. Once when I was sharing a room with him at a Crusader week-end, I saw him at 6 o'clock in the morning on his knees, with his Bible open and his prayer list — together with photographs — spread around him on the bed. There I learned his secret; he fed his own soul so effectively that there was always an overflow for the benefit of others.

There was also A DEEPENING FULFILMENT IN CHRIST. He might have said of Jesus what Helen Keller said of Anne Sullivan: "My teacher is so close to me that I can scarcely think of myself apart from her . . . All the best of me belongs to her — there is not a talent or an aspiration or a joy in me that has not been awakened by her loving touch." What was best in T.S. was awakened by the loving touch of Christ. He liked the words often quoted by the late John Davey.

"Nothing less do I require; nothing more can I desire.
None but Christ to me be given,
Christ for earth and Christ for heaven."

He could recall this prayer of Mr. White's:
"May a Dying Saviour's Love and a Risen Saviour's Life, and a Coming Saviour's Glory be the Joy of all our hearts and the Ground of all our confidence."

With Christ he found **A PURPOSE TO FULFIL.**

"For me to live is Christ." Wm. Barclay wrote: "A man must give his life to that which gave him life."

This brings DEDICATION. "Take all sense of dedication and purpose out of a man's life," said C. S. Lewis, "and he will become the obedient servant of hell."

There was his dedication as AN ELDER. For more than forty years he was an elder in the Great James' Street Congregation, which had such a warm place in his heart. As teacher and Bible-class leader, as Editor of the 'Messenger,' as Clerk of Session, as friend of the six ministers under whom he served, he made a unique contribution to the work. Traditionalist though he was, nothing gave him greater joy in recent years than to be part of the exciting new development at Kilfennan under the Minister

Rev. Edgar S. McKinney. But his vision was not limited to one congregation, or even to one Presbytery. How faithful he was in attending numerous Committees and Boards of the Church, and what wit and wisdom he brought to many of their discussions. He enjoyed the respect of a wide cross-section of members of the General Assembly. I shall not easily forget the wry smile and the sharp retort he gave me when I chided him with becoming 'the voice of the Establishment.'

There was his dedication as A WORKER. UCCF (IVF), the Portstewart Convention, the Qua Iboe Mission, the Christian Workers' Union (to which his lifelong friend, the late Mr. Joe Goligher, had introduced him), the local Auxiliary of the Bible Society, the Young People's Convention — all of them he served at one time or another as Hon. Treasurer, and all of them are in his debt. How thrilling for him to see Waterside Presbyterian Church packed last Sunday evening for the final meeting of the Convention, and how fitting that his final speech should have been on Monday at the Dinner to mark the fiftieth anniversary.

Then there was his dedication as A LEADER. Without doubt, some of his most rewarding work was done with his Crusader Class. J. T. Carson had some contact with the Belfast Class — the first in Northern Ireland — before coming to Magee in October 1930. Together J.T. and T.S. opened the Derry Class in November of that year, with an attendance of nine boys, and for fifty years T.S. was its leader. At the same time he played an increasing part in the work of the Crusader Movement throughout the province. His aim was, in his own words, "to give every boy a book in his hand, a Saviour in his heart and a purpose in his life." Interestingly enough, during the War years, the Crusader magazine reported that among those who offered hospitality to Crusaders serving in the Forces were Mr. & Mrs. T. S. Mooney. When told of this he said, "It's only a rumour."

There was also his dedication as A PREACHER. From his earliest years he had wanted to be a minister, but coming in second place in a vital scholarship examination after four years at Coleraine Inst., thwarted his desire to enter the University. This, however, was no failure, but rather the opening of a door to a unique life of service to men who trained at Magee College for the ministry of our Church. The warmth of his friendship, the open door of his home, and his happy knack of being able to win the confidence of young men enabled him to do more for the ministry than if he had been in the ministry. How many there are who had their thinking, and their preaching shaped by his wholesome teaching and his wise counsel. This, in part, opened many Manses and many pulpits to the elder from Derry. This was also true in Scotland. His preaching bore his own inimitable stamp: the epigrammatic style, the fine turn of phrase, the apt illustration — all this gave wings to the Gospel truth he rejoiced to proclaim. Over the years he ministered in more than one hundred of our pulpits — surely a record for an elder. And in it all he sought only to glory in the Cross of our Lord Jesus Christ. More than once I heard him quote Forsythe's words: "When the Cross goes out of the centre of religion, the preacher has too much to say and too little to tell."

Hand-in-hand with dedication went DISCIPLINE. From his appointment to the Bank in February, 1925 until his retirement in 1970, he never saw his work in the bank as a second-best to his work as a Christian. It taught him ways of self-discipline which he followed in every phase of life. Think of the hours spent in reading, prayer and preparation — and of those other hours spent on the road. One can say of T.S. what George Fox's biographer said of him: "he was completely the master of himself because he was completely the servant of God." I can recall him leaving our Manse in Kilkeel at 5.30 in the morning in order to be in the office before it opened. Christian service on Sunday was no excuse for half-hearted service on Monday. He was one who would never give in to himself for the sake of convenience. He might have said with Augustine: "To my God a heart aflame; to my fellow men a heart of love; and to myself a heart of steel."

Through Christ he found **A PROSPECT TO FACE.**

. . . to live is Christ, and to die is gain. He lived his life and did his work against the backdrop of eternity, strong in the conviction that "the best is yet to be."

This gave him SECURITY. I had a friend in Kilkeel, a Roman Catholic who, in the post-War years, worked as a junior with T.S. Often if T.S. were going to Belfast for the week-end he would give Maurice a lift. One Friday night they were hurtling along in the Sunbeam Rapier across the Glenshane Pass. Maurice was more than a little apprehensive. At last he said to T.S. "Mr. Mooney this may be alright for a good livin' man like you, but don't you think it's a little bit risky for the like of me?" T.S. enjoyed a security, as Maurice thought, better than that of any bank.

It also gave him EXPECTANCY. He dropped more than one hint in recent months that he was looking forward to going Home. He didn't speculate about the future. He was content to say with Richard Baxter: "My knowledge of that life is small; the eye of faith is dim. But 'tis enough that Christ knows all, and I shall be with him." On Friday last the end came suddenly just as he would have liked it to come.
"He was not, for God took him."

In words that he liked to quote:

> *"Night slipped to dawn and pain merged into beauty,*
> *Bright grew the road his faithful feet had trod;*
> *He gave his salutation to the morning*
> *And found himself before the Throne of God."*

As we look back, let us give thanks to God for such a life, but better still let us thank Him for the grace that made it possible. Let us express our sympathy with his sister, Margaret, and his nephews Nevin and Ray, and let us commend them to the God of all grace.

Perhaps we might ask ourselves: for me to live is? Have we found in Christ a Person to follow . . . a purpose to fulfil . . . a prospect to face?

A.F.

The Prayer

Almighty God, our Heavenly Father, we draw near to the Throne of Grace to-day in faith and in love. Only thus can we come when sorrows fill our hearts and perplexities our minds. We who were strong have been made conscious of our impotence. We who were so rich and adequate have become aware of our weakness and impoverishment. We who are so often self-assured have been thrown back on Thee for comfort and consolation. Therefore, in our need and weakness we draw near to Thee, O God of our salvation.

We bless Thy name, O Lord, that when our hearts are overwhelmed by the mysteries of life and of death, Thou art greater than our hearts, our refuge and our strength, our Father and our Friend.

We praise Thee for Thy loving kindness to us all and especially to-day to our dear friend, Thy good and worthy servant, Tom Mooney, now passed from our presence into Thine eternal joy. Humbly yet proudly and with unspeakable gratitude would we say this day "The Lord gave, The Lord hath taken away, Blessed be the name of the Lord."

We bless Thee for that gracious home into which he was born, that heritage of faith and devotion which he received there and which he was proud to acknowledge throughout the years.

We thank Thee that in his early days Thou didst sovereignly and savingly call him to thyself with an effectual calling. Thou didst order his steps in Thy word and call him into Thy glad service.

We bless thee that thou didst endow him with gifts and graces. Thou didst acknowledge his labours and so set thy seal upon him that all his life's journey was motivated by his concern for the kingdom of his Lord.

We glorify thee for all that he was in himself and for all that by grace he became. We thank thee that with him thou didst make an ambassador of Thy love and mercy, a constant witness to the fact that where Jesus comes miracles of salvation take place and where sin abounds grace can even much more abound.

We remember his own clear and honest faith in the Redeemer and his humble submission to Thine own infallible word. We recall his great concern to buy the truth and sell it not, and his delight in an uncluttered gospel preached with love and urgency. We thank thee for the untiring devotion which he brought to the study of thy Word and all the years he gave to the teaching of it, and for his restless eagerness for its distribution to the ends of the earth.

We remember his sense of duty and his faithfulness in the service of his God and his fellowmen. Being faithful in lesser things thou didst entrust him with duties that were demanding and responsible, and these he did with conscience and integrity. For his reputation in the work of his profession and the good name he had with all and sundry in business life, thy holy name be praised.

With special gratitude we remember the work he did for Christ and the Church in various spheres.

For his devotion to the Sunday School and to his Bible Class;

For the many years of self sacrificing work with which he served his Crusader Class;

For the wisdom of his experience which he shared with his brethren in the work of Presbytery and General Assembly, and for the humility, courtesy and tolerance which marked it all;

to God be all the Glory.

We thank Thee too, O God, for the example he set us in his undying concern for the salvation of the lost and perishing and the support he was ever ready to give to this glorious work, in his own city and throughout the countryside. And also, O God, for that hunger and thirst that he had that the utmost ends of the earth should see the salvation of God.

That this man could care so much and could accomplish so much was often a rebuke to our complacency but to-day O Lord, we remember with gratitude the encouragement he gave to us all and the constant inspiration which he was; let his influence remain with us. Thou hast said, 'He that winneth souls is wise and they that turn many to righteousness shall shine as the stars for ever and ever.' May this, which he both did and was, be a star to guide us too as we try to keep the memory of this good man alive in our hearts.

O God of the universal harvest, thou alone canst tell the true value of the work of any of Thy servants; be pleased to accept our thanks this day for the example he set and for the influence that he was, and for the harvest yet to be reaped, far beyond his knowledge or expectation, and in ways only thou dost know, the harvest that will be the fulfilment in the years to come of the service of the past. All glory, laud and honour, O Lord, be thine.

We would not forget, O Lord, to thank thee for all he was within his own family circle as a devoted son, and as a brother beloved. Remember then this day these Thy servants who are bereft of such a brother, and uncle, and cousin. For all his unrecorded acts of thoughtfulness and kindness, for his generosity to men and movements in the interests of the

Kingdom of God, and for the ministry of his pen and letters we praise Thy Name, O God.

And now, Lord God, Father of all mercies and God of all comfort, send thy consolations to all who share our loss to-day. Remember those who were his true yoke-fellows in the work of the Kingdom, his beloved brethren in Gt. James Street and Kilfennan, his friends in many congregations and in various denominations, in many walks in life, in this and every land. Remember too his successors in the Derry Crusader Class.

Into every circle do Thou send the healing of thy love. On every bereaved heart may there shine gleams of the splendour of that other world where Jesus is crowned with glory and honour, and where he is vested with the keys of life and of death forever. In thy mercy fill the gap thy servant leaves behind him. Raise up many more like him and prosper the work he loved and served.

O Lord Jesus Christ, thou didst die for us and rise again that we might live with thee forever, be Thou our salvation now and our rest when the shadows of the evening are stretched out and when our day is over, and our work is done, then O thou King of Angels, Saviour of sinners bring us to thyself.

Bring us, O Lord God, at our last awakening into the house and gate of heaven, to enter into that gate and dwell in that house where there shall be no darkness nor dazzling, but one heavenly light; no frightening noise nor eerie silence, but one divine music; no paralysing fears nor unfulfilled hopes, but one secure possession; no ends nor beginnings but one perfect eternity, in the dwelling place of thy glory and dominion, world without end. Till then, Beloved Father

O spread thy covering wings around
Till all our wanderings cease;
And at our Father's loved abode
Our souls arrive in peace.

All that we ask this day in our weakness, all that we bring this day in our thanksgiving, all that, in solemn vow, we would dedicate now, we offer in the dear name of our Lord Jesus Christ to whom be all the glory for ever and ever. AMEN.

J.T.C.

TO THE MEN WHO WOULD ASPIRE TO TAKE MR. GREATHEART'S PLACE

"After this it was noised abroad that Mr. VALIANT-FOR-THE-TRUTH (the man whom Greatheart thought would follow him) was sent for by summons . . . When he understood it he called for his friends and told them of it. Then he said, I am going to my Father's house; and though with great difficulty I have got hither, yet now I do not repent me of all the troubles I have been at to arrive where I am. My Sword I give to him that shall succeed me in my pilgrimage, and my courage and skill to him that can get it. My marks and scars I carry with me to be a witness for me that I have fought His battles who now will be my rewarder.

When the day was come, he passed over and all the trumpets sounded for him on the other side."

Castlerock Crusader Camp (c.1934) with some Portrush C.S.S.M. Party Visitors.
Seated: A. C. Anderson (Rev. Dr., Newcastle), ?, George Ross (Dr.), Kyle M. Alexander, (Rev., Portrush), T.S., Rev. W. G. Ovens, J. T. Carson (Rev. Dr., Ballymena and Bangor).
Others in the Group include Jim Fitzsimons (Rev., Portstewart), Rev. Canon S. May, R.A.E. Magee (Gynaecologist R.M.H.), Cecil Craig (Rev., Waringstown), David R. Wilkinson, (Barrister), Frank Williams (Rev., C. of I.), Gillie Smith (Rev., Canada), Ernie Smith (Rev.).

APPENDIX ONE

T.S. — In the Editor's Chair

When an artist has finished a painting, whether it is likely to be a valuable masterpiece or not, he invariably adds a signature or a sign to ensure that no charlatan or rogue will later get credit for it. About 1969 Mr. Mooney became the editor of the Great James St. Presbyterian Church's "Messenger" although for years before that he served on the Editorial Committee under Principal Guthrie of Magee College and made occasional contributions to it.

From 1969 he was firmly in the Editor's chair, yet never once did his name appear, either as editor or as the writer of the editorials. These were, of course, so characteristic of T.S., in style, vocabulary and subject that they did not need a name attached to indicate who the author was. The congregation knew and these scribblings were so highly valued that the opinion was often expressed that they deserved a wider readership. This memoir provides an opportunity for this to be done and the following are a small selection from a much wider collection stretching back for many years.

Fencing the Table   MAY 1970

"Fencing the Table". What an odd expression that is! Yet it was one quite familiar to Presbyterians in connection with the Communion Service and it stood for something really important. After the main address — generally known as the "action sermon" — the minister came down to the Table and instructed intending communicants on the qualifications required for the "worthy receiving" of the Lord's Supper. This was known as "fencing the Table". One purpose of a fence is to exclude, and such an idea relative to the Lord's Table has Scriptural sanction. It applied to the original institutions of the Passover. "There shall no stranger eat thereof". (Ex. 12: 43) and now that the memorial feast of God's ancient people has been replaced by the Lord's

87

Supper the same principle applied. "He that eateth and drinketh unworthily, eateth and drinketh judgment to himself" (I Cor. 11: 29). So in both Testaments we have the "fencing of the Table".

But a fence may be either too high or too low. It may be so high that **nobody** may come in or so low that **anybody** may come in, and both these defects have from time to time appeared in the Church. Ian Maclaren, in one of his Scottish stories, relates how an old minister of the High Calvinist School "spoke to the communicants and distinguished the true people of God from the multitude by so many and stringent marks that Donald Menzies — one of the saintliest men in the congregation — refused the sacrament with a lamentable groan". And Dr. Norman Maclean tells how, due to an extreme form of such teaching, "the Table of the Lord was unfurnished with guests and Communion Rolls were reduced from hundreds to under ten" for even the godliest of men felt unfitted for the high privilege of sitting at Christ's Table. Perhaps they needed to hear Dr. John Duncan's words to the woman who with tears refused the Cup and pased it to her neighbour. Bringing it back to her Duncan said in homely Doric "Tak it wuman, it's for sinners". And so it is — but for sinners who are conscious of their sin, and, therefore, of their need of a Saviour.

When Charles Simeon as an undergraduate at Cambridge heard that he must communicate at the Easter celebration of Holy Communion in his college chapel he was alarmed "for", said he, "the devil himself was as fit to attend as I". His distress of mind led him to read Bishop Wilson's book on the Lord's Supper and there he came upon a sentence that led him into the light. "The Jews", wrote the good bishop, "knew what they did when they transferred their sins to the head of a sin-offering". "Accordingly", confesses Simeon, "I sought to lay my sins upon the sacred head of Jesus. On Easter Day I was enabled to see that all my sins were buried in my Redeemer's grave and at the Lord's

---

MOONEYISM

Those who come to the Lord's Table saying, "We would see Jesus" never go away disappointed.

Table in our chapel I had the sweetest access to God through my blessed Saviour".

So for the young Cambridge undergraduate the way to a "worthy receiving" of the Lord's Supper lay in a personal faith in the blood of his Redeemer. It is thus that we too shall find the way through "the fence" for it is as true of the Lord's Table as it is of heaven itself that—

> There was no other good enough
> To pay the price of sin
> He only could unlock the gate
> . . . and let us in.

Come Wind, Come Weather FEBRUARY 1970

It was a dark, wet, winter morning. The rain was coming down in sheets and the wind was blowing it in waves along the street. But the girls on their way to start work in the factory at 8 o'clock were making the best of it. They had their job to do and **the weather didn't matter.**

A concert had been arranged and soloists, nationally known for their vocal gifts, were to be on the programme. The tickets had sold like hot cakes and everybody who was anybody had planned to be there. The chosen date turned out to be an evening of rain and sleet and biting cold. But the large concert hall was filled to capacity. There were celebrated soloists to be heard and **the weather didn't matter.**

His Grace the Governor and his lady were visiting the city, and a dinner in their honour was being given in the City Hall. Invitations had been sent to all leading citizens and they had almost all indicated their intention of being present. From a weather point of view the evening was most unpleasant and the wind and rain threatened to play havoc with the finery of the Mayor's guests. But they all turned up. It was an important civic and social occasion and **the weather didn't matter.**

It was a Sunday evening. The church doors were open, a service had been announced, and the King of Kings had indicated his intention of being present. He had ordained that one of His servants should tell those who gathered the good news of what the King proposed to do for them in this world and the next. But the night was wet and windy, the fireside was warm and cheery, and listening to the wintry blast as it howled in the chimney Mr. Churchmember said to his wife; "I don't think we'll go to church to-night, dear. In such weather it would be pleasant to sit by the fire and watch the TV". "Yes indeed", his wife replied, "it's much too wet and cold to get out the car and we might get our feet wet going up the church steps and catch this awful 'flu that's going around".

So when the King came in to see His subjects who had gathered to meet Him and to hear His herald proclaim the good news of his Master's generosity there were but a few people present, many of them no longer young. Then said the King to His servant: "I am glad to see these loyal subjects of mine, but where are all the others who have sworn an oath of allegiance to Me so often at My Table"? "Well, you see Master", the servant replied, "it is a wet evening and when it is a matter of meeting You and hearing one of Your proclamations **weather matters so very much**".

A Thermometer or a Thermostat?
MARCH 1975

Inside one of the vestibule doors at the church there hangs a small thermometer which indicates the temperature of the building at any particular time. Sometimes on a wintry Sunday we might wish that it registered a higher figure than it does but, cold or hot, the thermometer simply takes its cue from the state of the atmosphere around it. Attached to some heating systems, however, there is a thermostat, the purpose of which is to control the amount of heat. Should the temperature rise too high it switches the system off. Should it drop below a certain figure it switches it on again. The thermometer simply records the state of the atmosphere; the thermostat regulates it.

Christian people fall into these two classes. There are those who simply reflect the kind of moral and spiritual surroundings in which they move. "When in Rome" they say "you must do as the Romans do". Young folk feel that they must be "with it" and older folk don't want to be regarded as "eccentric", so the things that are central to the life of the wordlings around them must be central for them too. There are, however, thank God, other

Christians who feel that it is more important to be loyal to Christ than to "keep up with the Joneses" and who seek to influence the community rather than allow themselves to be influenced by it. And so there is the contrast between the thermometers and the thermostats.

An incident in the life of the Apostle Peter gives us a good example of "the thermometer Christian". When his Master, under arrest, was taken for judgment to the High Priest's Palace Peter, instead of pressing into the courtroom and keeping as close to Christ as possible so as to be available for any service he could render, remained outside in the courtyard. There he strolled over and sat down amongst a group around a brazier. Their sneers at the Prisoner and their jokes at His expense went unchallenged by His disciple, and so Peter denied Christ by his silence thus making almost inevitable the denial in words that followed.

Fortunately, however, Scripture is not without instances of the other kind and perhaps one of the best is the story of what we call the "three Hebrew children". They were young fellows in a hostile environment to the influence of which many of their fellow-Jews succumbed. When a heathen king issued a command that everyone should bow down and worship the golden image set up, by royal decree, all the other Jews in the crowd apparently complied. They may have bowed with regret — or with mental reservations! — but down they went with the idolatrous crowd around them. There were, however, three young lads "with no hinges to their knees" and their upright figures were conspicuous amongst their supine companions. The rest of the story, well known to every reader of the Book of Daniel, shows how their conduct influenced a whole heathen community and emphasises how much better it is to be a thermostat than a thermometer.

This is still a live issue. The days in which we live with their social pressures and a permissive society with its lowering standards, are a constant temptation to compromise.

Cowardice asks is it safe? Convention, is it polite?

Vanity asks is it popular? But conscience asks is it right?

And my loyalty to conscience and to Christ will determine whether I'm to be the salt of the earth and the light of the world — a thermostat or merely a thermometer.

91

Well-wishers or Warriors?   OCTOBER 1978

A Scottish preacher commenting on Gideon's Army of 32,000 and its subsequent reduction to 300 remarked that the cause of Jesus Christ has never lacked its well-wishers but soldiers ready to stand the test of the day of battle are a scarcer breed. No one who knows anything of the realities of church life will question that statement. There are many who value the church's influence for good in the community, who are glad to hear encouraging reports at annual congregational meetings and who would regret exceedingly the elimination of the church's witness from our national life — but that is as far as it goes. They are a kind of supporters' club rather than playing members of the team.

Many people for example attend the Schools' Cup rugby match at Ravenhill on St. Patrick's Day. They are not interested in the result, they know which side they wish to win and their sympathies are often given strenuous vocal expression, but in the end of the day the result owes nothing to them. They were only on the touch-line and not really involved in the hotly-contested game. So it is in the spiritual realm. The religion of the touch-line is a poor substitute for Christian commitment. A caustic critic of modern church life has described many congregations as "the members standing on the touch-line as spectators, the session and a few others playing their hearts out and the minister trying to keep goals — and score them at the same time!" In that connection Michael Griffiths, a missionary statesman of our time, has written "any fool can shout abuse and offer unsolicited advice from the grandstand. What we need are Christians who will get their heads into the church scrum and shove".

It is sadly true that the last thing many so-called church members want is personal involvement in Christ's cause in the world. As Sir John Lawrence writing in "Frontier" has put it "What does the average layman really want? He wants a building which looks like a church, a clergyman dressed in the way he approves, services of the kind he has been used to — and to be left alone". But the battle for the Kingdom can never be won on these terms. Dr. A. L. Griffiths was much nearer the mark when in one of his sermons he told his people in the City Temple — "In some churches the parson instructs and the people learn. All that is required is that they be in their places on time. Other churches are like religious theatres where worshippers come to enjoy a professional performance which must please the audience. Others are like clubs which exist for the benefit of those who belong to them. Instead they should be battle-training schools from which the highly trained and dedicated nucleus sallies forth to fight the Lord's battles". To win that fight we need not well-wishers but warriors.

Communion Reflections NOVEMBER 1978

For many years the last Sabbath in October has been the day of the Autumn Communion in the Presbyterian churches of this city. Consequently most of those who read these words will have sat once again at the Lord's Table to remember the Saviour's dying and deathless love in the way of His own appointment. Some will have sat there for the first time, some perhaps for the last time, and for all it has been a time of privilege and opportunity. Just as "beauty lies in the eye of the beholder" so the Lord's Supper may be anything from an empty religious formality to a little bit of heaven upon earth, according to the spiritual eyesight of the communicant. What should we see in the communion service anyhow?

Well, for one thing we should find in it **a profile.** An American library possess a copy of the Declaration of Independence printed in such a way that, viewed from the right angle, it shows an outline of the features of George Washington. So, looked at with the eyes of faith and love, the Lord's Supper displays the lineaments of a suffering Saviour. "This is my body broken"; "This is my blood shed". As Horatius Bonar has it in the hymn of the Sacrament Sabbath: "Here, oh my Lord, I see Thee face to face". "In the Word", said Robert Bruce in his great book on this subject, "I get Christ by my ear, but in the Supper I get Christ by my eye". Those who come to His Table praying "We would see Jesus" never go away disappointed.

Then in the sacrament there is a **profession.** No man who has ever sat at Christ's Table can ever say again "I make no profession of being religious". Our word "sacrament" comes not from Scripture but from the early centuries of Church history when the Latin word "sacramentum," meaning an oath of allegiance, was applied by converted Roman soldiers to the sacramental feast. So all who have ever participated in a Communion service have sworn an oath of allegiance to Christ to be "true-hearted, whole-hearted, faithful and loyal" till their life's end. Being a communicant is as compelling and as comprehensive as that.

Best of all at the Lord's Table we experience "the rapture of the forward view" for we "show the Lord's death **till He come"**, and therefore in it we find **a prophecy** of a gladsome day yet to be. So

"Feast after feast thus comes and passes by,
Yet, passing, points to that glad feast above;
Giving sweet foretaste of the festal joy,
The Lamb's great bridal feast of bliss and love".

What a Communion Service that will be and what will it be to be there?" "Aye", as Dr. Alexander Whyte once said. "and what will it be **not** to be there"?

"Be Careful with that T.V. Set" MAY 1979

Amongst the many good gifts with which God, through the men of science, has enriched the life of this generation are surely to be numbered wireless and television. Yet man's sinful nature too often leads him to abuse the gifts and forget the Giver, thus turning what might have been a blessing into what may well be a curse. In these days when a higher standard of living has enabled almost every home to have its T.V. set, some counsels need to be laid to heart if God's gift is not to become the enemy of God's will. Of these counsels we suggest three:-

1. **Don't let T.V. monopolise your time.** In too many homes it has replaced all intelligent conversation and all serious reading.

MOONEYISM

The greatest tragedy of all is that these terrible years have failed to bring the Church in Ulster to its knees in earnest, united and importunate prayer. Church courts have passed resolutions. Church leaders have made pronouncements. Ministers have preached impressive sermons at funeral services, but the Church has not given itself to prayer.

Common courtesy also falls a victim to its influence, and the failure to switch off the set even when the minister calls makes true pastoral visitation and a pastoral prayer well-nigh impossible. See to it, therefore, that T.V. is the servant and not the master in your house.

2. **Don't let T.V. lower your moral standards.** Choose with care the programmes which you and your family watch. Too often the ubiquitous glass on the screen provides a free advertisement for the liquor trade while other commodities have to pay for their publicity. The violence which is an integral part of many plays, the smutty jokes and the vulgarity which some artistes mistake for humour should be avoided like the plague, for foul germs in the soul are much more dangerous than those which kill the body.

3. **Don't let T.V. secularise your Sundays.** The Sabbath is God's holy day and we desecrate it at our own and our children's peril. The question, therefore, to ask about the television fare provided for Sundays is "Will this programme make the Lord's Day more secular or more sacred?" The answer to that question will give a Christian man infallible guidance as to whether his T.V. set should be switched on or switched off. It is a solemn thought that the spiritual welfare of a whole household may depend upon whether a knob is turned clockwise or anti-clockwise — but then "great doors swing on small hinges".

The following "continuous viewer's version" of the 23rd Psalm may sound somewhat extreme but there is enough truth in it to make us all think and perhaps persuade us to "be careful with that T.V. set":—

"The T.V. set is my shepherd; my spiritual growth shall want.

"It maketh me to sit down and do nothing for His Name's sake, because it requireth all my spare time.

"It keepeth me from doing my duty as a Christian because it presenteth so many good things that I MUST see.

"It restoreth my knowledge of the things of the world, and easily keepeth me from the study of God's Word.

"It leadeth me in the paths of failing to attend the evening worship services, and doeth nothing for the Kingdom of God.

"Yea, though I live to be a hundred, I shall keep on viewing my T.V. as long as it will work, for it is my closest companion.

"Its sounds and its pictures they comfort me.

"It presenteth entertainment before me, and keepeth me from doing important things with my family.

"It can easily (if I am not careful . . . and that would involve effort and thought) fill my head with ideas which are opposed to those of Christ.

"Surely no good thing will come to my life, because my T.V. offereth me no time to do the Will of God; thus will I dwell in the house which is not God's for ever."

What is a Christian? OCTOBER 1985

One could hardly ask a more important question that that and yet the answers of many people would often be very vague indeed. The Bishop of Chelmsford describes much religious thinking as "frothy religious sentiment" and suggests that its creed runs something like this:—

"I believe in God the Father because I feel sure there must be a God of some kind, a sort of eternal good nature and easy-going tolerance.

"I believe that Jesus Christ lived a holy life which I ought to imitate. I have great reverence for the Cross but I do not pretend to understand what it means.

"I am not quite sure whether I believe in life everlasting but if there is such a thing I believe everything will turn out alright for everybody; at any rate I hope so. Amen."

Others would say that Christianity implies a certain moral standard and an edition of Webster's Dictionary once described a Christian as "a decent, civilized or respectable person." Some would claim that if a man has a certain amount of religious knowledge — The Lord's Prayer and some Cup-final hymns — then he could claim the name Christian. Those with an ecclesiastical turn of mind would say that he must have a connection with a church. A great German theologian, however, once said that the difference between the Roman and the Reformed churches was that the former said "If you're not in the Church you're not in Christ" while the latter declares "If you're not in Christ you're not in the Church." It would appear then that a Christian is — to use Paul's phrase — "a man in Christ," and that, it would seem, implies three things — believing, belonging and behaving, and they come in that order.

The believing that starts a man on the Christian life is not merely intellectual assent to a creed — important and all as that is. Perhaps the word that gets closer to the heart of the matter is the word "trust" or "faith" and there is no better definition of faith than the answer given to question 86 in the Shorter Catechism "Faith in Jesus Christ is a saving grace whereby we receive and rest upon Him alone for salvation as He is offered to us in the Gospel." This is sometimes summarised in an acrostic,

"Forsaking All I Take Him."

A. M. Toplady was a Church of England clergyman who wrote a great hymn which we know as "Rock of Ages." To take down our hymnbook and speak to God in Toplady's words is, if the words come from the heart, to pray the prayer of saving faith. As the last verse of the 46th Paraphrase has it:

"Jesus how glorious is thy grace,
When in Thy name we trust
Our faith receives a righteousness
That makes the sinner just.

Then believing is followed by belonging. 1 Cor. 6: 19, 20. "Ye are not your own. Ye are brought with a price. "So a Christian is not merely a man who obeys Paul's words to the Philippian jailor "Believe on the Lord Jesus Christ and thou shalt be saved" but he also belongs to Christ. Paul delights to describe himself as "the bondslave of Jesus Christ" and as we seek to emulate him in this we find that bondage to Christ is perfect freedom.

All this leads us by the help of the Holy Spirit to behaving like Christ. "I saw a saint today" writes Christina Rossetti "How knowest thou that he thou sawest was a saint?" "He was like Christ so luminously." This likeness will not come suddenly. Indeed such growth in grace is the work of a lifetime. Like Paul we must be ever "pressing toward the mark" and so believing, belonging and behaving we sing with Charles Wesley.

"Ready for all thy perfect will.
My acts of faith and love repeat
Till death thy endless mercies seal
and make the sacrifice complete."

T.S.: The Committee man

The two "Appendices" which follow will show clearly how seriously Mr. Mooney took the responsibilities and duties of a Presbyterian elder. It seemed apt that some idea might be given here of how faithfully he followed out his own rules, and the following list of the Committees and Boards of the General Assembly, to which he was appointed after his retirement from the Bank in 1971. It should be remembered that membership of any committee was never nominal only; he endeavoured to attend as well. Even this list does not include his involvement in the affairs of Conventions, United Colleges Christian Unions (U.C.C.F.) Temperance and Missionary bodies.

Doctrine Committee
Southern Committee
Church Extension Committee
State of Religion and Evangelisation
Arrangements Committee
Moderator's Advisory Committee
Belfast/Derry Committee
Racism Committee
Board Appointments Committee
Recognised Ministries Committee
City Area Committee
Union Theological College Management
Special *ad hoc* Committee on Theological Education
Special *ad hoc* Committee on the Eldership
The Overseas Board
Business Board
Board of Finance and Administration
Board of Studies
The Union Commission
A Trustee of Magee University College
A Trustee of the Presbyterian Church in Ireland

Council of the Presbyterian Historical Society of Ireland
Chairman of the Presbyterian Fellowship since its
    foundation in 1961

APPENDIX TWO

"The Eldership"

From four talks given to the Kirk Session of St. David's Parish Church, Knightswood, Glasgow, at the Gean House, Alloa, 7th-9th October, 1966 and to several other gatherings of elders. They have been ably reduced in size and in this form by Rev. Malcolm Hare, St. Kentigern's Church of Scotland, Kilmarnock, Ayrshire . . . [Editor].

Perhaps we should talk generally about the subject of the Elder of the Kirk under four headings, namely (i) the kind of office he holds, (ii) the kind of man he ought to be, (iii) the kind of work he does, and (iv) the kind of ideals he cherishes. And as we do I suppose it is fitting that I pray the public speaker's prayer:

'Lord, fill my mind with worth-while stuff,
And nudge me hard when I've said enough!'

I speak to you as an evangelical Christian, as an ecumenical Christian — in the best sense of that word — and also as a Presbyterian Christian. I would hope I would neither be a cynic, who sees no good inside his own church, nor a bigot, who sees no good outside it; but for all that I agree with Professor T. H. Witherow who maintained that while you can be a Christian without being a Presbyterian and a Presbyterian without being a Christian, it is better to be both! I would be neither spineless nor spikey but still believing, even in these ecumenical days, that it is not a sin to say that one is a Presbyterian.

The Kind of Office He Holds

It is an *ancient* office, referred to in Mosaic times (Exod 4:29) and post-exilic times (Ezra 10:14), with a religious function in contrast to the judges whose function was a civil one. There are references to them in the Gospels where elders of Israel were associated with the High Priest, and not to their credit, in their attitude to Christ. You find references to them in the early days of the Church as we have it in the Acts of the Apostles, e.g. 11:30, 14:23, and in the Epistles, e.g., Tit. 1:5 and 1 Tim. 5:17. According to Rev. 4:4 there are elders in Heaven in the General Assembly of the Church of the First-born. So it is an ancient office; our place

99

is in the long line of men who stood in God's presence for men and men's presence for God.

It is a *Scriptural* office; at least in principle many of our practices today are justified by references in Acts and the Epistles. First, there is the idea of popular election. Acts 6:56, 14:23 show that church officers, including elders, were chosen by the people. Second, there is the plurality of elders. In every church in the early days there were always quite a number of them (Tit. 1:5). Third, there is no difference between 'bishop' and 'presbyter' in the Early Church. References in the works of Bishops Lightfoot, Moule, and Professor H. E. W. Turner show that these were but different names for different functions performed by the same people. According to Acts 20:28 the Holy Ghost had made them 'overseers' over the flock, some with gifts to rule, others with gifts to labour in the Word and doctrine. 1 Tim. 5:17 is the key verse concerning the difference between the preaching and ruling elder.

The eldership is a *Spiritual* office, as is seen from his appointment and his assignment. The Code of our Irish Presbyterian Church states that having oversight of the flock he is termed 'bishop', but as requiring to be grave and prudent in guiding and governing the church he is termed 'presbyter' or 'elder.' These different titles are applied to the same officers withour marking any superiority or difference of rank. All elders were apostolic bishops and held their commission from Christ. All elders ruled, some labouring in the Word and doctrine. Hence the titles 'Teaching Elder' and 'Ruling Elder.' The Scottish view is somewhat different from that today, but the Irish view has a long and honourable history even in Scotland itself and Professor Cheyne of New College Edinburgh is of the opinion that it is entitled to its place in Presbyterianism.[1]

The implication of this for today is three-fold. First, it affects *our view of the ministry*. The teaching elder's ministry is the ministry of the Word and everything else is secondary. The word 'priest' is never applied to him in the New Testament and Sacraments do not bear in Scripture the emphasis that is put upon them in many quarters today. It is right that the dispensing of Sacraments should be in the hands of recognised officers of the

[1] In an article in the New College Bulletin.

Church but this is merely a rule of good order. It is not a necessity. Priestcraft and Sacramentarianism always go together and an emphasis upon them is unhealthy as far as evangelical religion is concerned. We may not use the words but in some quarters the idea is not very far away. The Christian Ministry is the highest office on earth, the greatest task to which a man may be appointed but you don't increase its importance, or raise it in any way, by making claims for it that don't bear the authority of Holy Writ.

Second, *our idea of bishops* will also be affected. It was not until the Second Century that the three-fold ministry of bishops, priests, and deacons, was established. As late as 96A.D. Clement of Rome was speaking of 'bishops' and 'presbyters' as interchangeable terms for the same office. Professor H. E. W. Turner in his booklet 'Why Bishops?' after reviewing the New Testament evidence, comes to this (for some rather disappointing) conclusion; 'we have not been able to find clear, biblical, warrant for diocesan bishops.' Episcopacy, therefore, cannot be said, with any New Testament warrant, to be of the very essence of the Christian Church. I cannot see then why an office for which there is no clear scriptural warrant should be insisted upon as a necessary basis for Church unity.

Third, it also affects *our view of ourselves;* and about this there must be no presumption. As of the office of the High Priest in the old dispensation so it must be of the office of the eldership in the new; 'no man taketh this honour unto himself!' (Heb. 5:4). It is only the Holy Spirit in the long run who makes a man an elder. A Presbytery may or may not lay its hands on his head but unless the Holy Spirit has brought to bear His influence on his heart, the man is not really, in a New Testament sense, an elder.

The Kind of Man an Elder ought to Be

He will not be a perfect man, any more than Peter was. He played a large part in the history of the Early Church yet he was the man who denied our Lord. An elder won't be an infallible man, for Peter wasn't infallible, not even after Pentecost. Paul didn't believe in Peter's infallibility and I am inclined to think that those who claim to be Peter's successors are no more infallible than he was!

At the same time there are certain things that characterize an elder. First, he must be a man with *an experience* (1 Pet. 1:3, 23). Creed and conduct are connected by conversion and if you and I are to have any part not only in the eldership but even in the membership of the Christian Church we must have had an experience of coming to Christ, an experience of new Birth. Before a man can be in the Church at all he must be in Christ; and that can only come about by an experience of conversion. "While an educated ministry is desirable, a converted ministry is essential", stated a report of the Synod of Ulster. What is said of the teaching elder is equally true of the ruling elder. While an intelligent, wise, competent, eldership is desirable, a converted eldership is essential.

Then he must be a man with *a passion* (2 Pet. 1:1), a passion for Christ as His bondslave, belonging utterly and entirely to Christ. A man may be sound as to orthodoxy, churchmanship, and morality and not be a converted man. The one infallible sign that a man has passed from death to life is a passion for Christ and an intense loyalty to the Saviour.

An elder is a man who is *different* (1 Pet. 4:4). The world cannot succeed in squeezing him into its mould. There is a quality about his life which the world cannot understand. If you and I have never been laughed at for our Christianity the question is, have we any Christianity worth laughing at? If we are not a puzzle to the world, if they don't think us queer in certain ways, if they don't find things hard to explain in our character and conduct, then the question is, have we any real relationship to the Lord Jesus Christ? Hugh Miller once said, 'We influence men more by the way in which we differ from them than the ways in which we resemble them'. If a man really belongs to Christ he is bound to be different from those who know not the Saviour.

Next, he will be *a man of the Book.* To him the Bible will be finally and fully authoritative and the application of the Bible to his life will be real and practical (1 Pet. 3:10-12). If you and I are not walking Bibles then we are walking libels! "What should they know of England who only England know?" asked the poet, and there is a sense, what do they know of the Bible who only the Bible know? If we read the Bible we will want to read other things as well. We will want to know something of the story of the Church's life and the system of the Church's doctrine that forms the Church's Creed. I can suggest no better way in which ordinary mortals can get a good grip of the Church's doctrine than by a good knowledge of the Shorter Catechism.

Finally, an elder will be *a man of prayer* (1 Pet. 4:7), having a time for prayer, a place for prayer, and a purpose in prayer. Like his Master he will pray for the Church in general (Jn. 17:20) and individuals in particular (Lk. 22:31). As Robert Murray M'Cheyne said very truly, "What a man is upon his knees before God, that he is and nothing more."

All these things should characterize the man who has accepted the office of elder. Lamenting the fact that very few have reached such a point will get us nowhere. The only thing that will be of any practical use is that we should measure up to this standard as far as ordinary men, by the Grace of God, can.

The Kind of Work He Does

There are three spheres in which the elder will be conspicuously active; in the congregation, in the courts of the Church, and in the community that surrounds the church.

In the *congregation* he will do three things. First, *he supports his minister*, behind his back, which is where criticisms are generally voiced; to his face, because the work of the Ministry is often difficult and discouraging work in which spiritual results can be slow in coming and a word of encouragement can be a great help; and before the Throne of Grace, for that minister is a happy man who is surrounded by a Session who carry his name on their heart and mention it in their prayers.

Second, *he shepherds the flock,* as Peter urged (1 Pet. 5:2) and Paul advised (Acts 20;28). That means feeding the hungry by speaking a word in season to troubled souls, teaching in Sabbath School, or helping run the Bible Class. It means protecting the threatened — those threatened by temptation, those threatened by false cults and those threatened by stealers of sheep. It means retrieving the lost (Heb. 13:17), for souls are not just to be won, they are to be watched over. There can be few more salutary experiences than to read over old roll-books, for while there we find for our encouragement names that we feel certain are in the Book of Life, we find others which remind us of early promise unfulfilled and conscience challenges us as to how far we are personally to blame for that lack of fulfilment.

103

Third, *he sets an example* (1 Pet. 5:3) He will support his own church and its services, Sunday and Mid-week, in every way within his power (as the old C.E. Pledge put it) proving himself worthy of the office to which he is ordained. Not only by his loyalty but also by his liberality he will set an example to the flock. Meanness is a sin of which a Christian man should never be guilty. What we give is often a tip rather than a tithe and there are Christians who put in the plate on Sunday what they wouldn't put under a plate in a hotel or restaurant.

The Bible teaches that we give to God as God has prospered us and a man's attitude to money is the evidence of the state of his heart towards God. An elder should be an example not only in his loyalty to the House of God but in his liberality to the work of God.

He has work to do in *the courts of the Church* too, in the General Assembly and the Presbytery when he is elected to membership of them, and in the Kirk Session of which he is a permanent member. Some adopt a distant and critical attitude to the superior courts of the Church: but if things do not go there as he would like, it could be due to elders not taking their share in the humdrum work of the Church.

In the Kirk Session elders should seek the *unity* of the Session and for that to happen attention should be paid to what Paul says in Eph. 4:1-3. He should have a sense of responsibility, 'walk worthy'. Walk worthy of your high vocation and don't let anything small, or mean, or ignoble, mar your life and conduct, particularly in your membership of the Session. 'Pride is the root of all sins' and lies at the root of much disunity in the Church, not least in its courts. And forebearance; it would help us to put up with other people if occasionally we stopped to think of how much they had to put up with from us! We've got to remember that and so with responsibility, humility and forebearance with each other, we seek, as Scripture commands us, to keep the unity of the Spirit in the bond of peace, the spiritual unity that is very necessary to success in spiritual work.

And he will be concerned about the *spirituality* of the Session. Material things do have to be considered but the business of the Session is with the spiritual well-being of the congregation.

He will also seek the *vitality* of the Session, which can only come from the power of the Holy Spirit; and the best contribution we can make to that is to ensure that we ourselves are walking with God day by day, seeking afresh the enduement of the Holy Spirit. In this way we will make our own special contribution to the spirituality, and the vitality of this most important court of the Church.

We live in the world and the elder has a job to do in the *community* that surrounds the church. Our influence there, according to the Master, is to be that of salt to prevent rottenness and light to scatter darkness. Christian men are needed in the body politic today. We should have an influence in the business world by our integrity and our generosity, going the second mile in matters that astound the unbeliever. Most important of all, we should have an evangelistic influence because an elder meets men that his minister never meets and can make contacts his minister cannot make. All around us today are people enacting the tragedy of a Christless life and going to the still greater tragedy of a Christless eternity. God have mercy upon us if they see nothing in us and hear nothing from us that would save them from such a fate as that.

The Kind of Ideals He Cherishes

As someone has said, 'Ideals are like the stars; you can't reach them but you mustn't cease to steer by them' and that is so true of the ideals of our eldership.

First of all, there is *his own Christian character* (2 Pet. 1:5-8) It has been said that character is what a man is in the dark, that side of his life known only to himself and to God. In Hexham Abbey, Northumberland there is a memorial to a merchant bearing these words;

> *His heart was rich of such fine mould,*
> *that if you sowed therein the seeds of hate,*
> *it blossomed charity.*

A character like that will make a great impression inside the church and outside it. A truly Christian man will be respected by those who are not Christians and who may have no use for the Church as such.

Then, the ideals concerning *his home*. Scripture has something to say about this — 1 Tim. 3:4-5. Our relationship to our own family is the first and foremost of our responsibilities. Happy the young folk sent out into the world with the memory of a home where God is honoured and the things that are pure, lovely, and of good report are given first place. An elder has a responsibility to his friends also. His is a home that must be given to hospitality (1 Tim. 3:2). The elder, whether ruling or teaching, is not to be selfish in the use of the home God has given him, but to ensure that it is a means of grace to others, influencing them for the best things, a means of bringing them to Christ.

There are ideals to cherish *the Church* in general and his own church in particular. According to Eph. 5:25-27 the Church is to be without spot, free from sin, and without wrinkle, free from senility for wrinkles are the mark of age! We are to aim at the purity of the Church in life and doctrine, maintaining the enthusiasm that characterized our early days. The Church is to hold forth the Word as well as to hold fast the Word. It will be evangelical and evangelistic — with fire in its heart and wings on its feet. It will not merely be a pleasure steamer for those already on board, but a life-boat for those struggling with the waves.

Finally, there are the ideals so far as the permanence of *his own influence* is concerned. 2 Pet. 1:15 enshrines a principle that applies to all of us, the ideal that, when we are no longer here, such should have been the quality of our lives that an influence will abide in the lives of others after we have gone. In Dornoch Cathedral there is this tribute to a former Duchess of Sutherland

> *Her name is in the hearts of those*
> *Who have been blessed to call her friend,*
> *To blossom like a fragrant rose*
> *Until their lives shall end.*

That sets before us an ideal for our own personal influence, that, we should so live, like Christ and for Christ, that our influence over others shall abide in their lives long after we have joined the Church Triumphant.

That is the ideal we must cherish and we shall only manage to achieve it, as to achieve any ideal in the Christian life, through the Grace that is in Christ Jesus, through dependence upon Him Who says 'My grace is sufficient for thee', through our reliance upon the Holy Spirit every day we live and through a diligent use of the Means of Grace. If we are men of prayer and men of the Book, then the Master's prayer will be answered for us, 'Sanctify them through thy truth: Thy word is truth.' (Jn. 17:17).

It seems to me, as Tennyson has it —

'Tis only noble to be good,
Kind hearts are more than coronets,
And simple faith than Norman blood.

And likeness to Christ is the best characteristic of them all.

He was often asked to propose a vote of thanks to 'the ladies' and he often did so, saying inter alia, *"The Ladies! The Lord bless them and* keep *them. I have no hesitation in giving them the right hand of fellowship but I keep them at arm's length*

Asked, as he often was, why he never married, he frequently explained that "the attainable was not always desirable, and the desirable was not always attainable."

But he also, loved to say, "If for no other reason than to keep him humble, every minister needs a wife."

He thought there was a lot of sense in Bishop Chadwick's comment in his book on the Johannine Epistles, "There are popes in surplices, popes in Genevan gowns, popes in frock coats and popes in petticoats."

A man in his Bible Class once told him that he had a dream in which he found himself in Heaven among lots of people in white robes. "Away down the line I saw you, Mr. Mooney. Do you know how I knew you? You wore your crown at an angle."

APPENDIX III

Zion's Courts

One of the characteristics of Presbyterianism as we know it is its system of graded Courts, of which in our Church there are four, Kirk Session, Presbytery, Synod and General Assembly. (Some cynical people say there is a fifth called "Church House", but nobody takes that seriously!) The Session is mostly concerned with the affairs of the local Congregation. The Synod has unfortunately become somewhat of a spare wheel in our ecclesiastical machinery, so that it is to the Presbytery and General Assembly that in this article we will direct our attention. By these Courts the Church is governed and their doings and decisions are therefore a matter of general concern to all lovers of our Presbyterian Zion.

Yet there are good men, Ministers and Elders, who take little interest in Church Courts and seldom attend them. Indeed it was one of the greatest of Scottish preachers of the last generation who said that he only went to Presbytery once a year. He went once to preserve his Presbyterianism, and only once to preserve his Christianity! And his biographer quotes Dr. James MacGregor of St. Cuthbert's, Edinburgh, as saying, "I go into Presbytery a humble Christian man and I come out an incarnate devil". Both instances go to prove that even good men and great Ministers are not infallible.

Too busy!

One of the duties a Minister at his Ordination promises to undertake is "aiding in the government of the Church" and that comes in the same question as that dealing with his other main duties as a Minister of the Gospel. In the same breath, therefore, he promises not only to be a faithful preacher and a zealous pastor, but also a good presbyter. If then he neglects the duties imposed by his membership of Presbytery and General Assembly he is breaking his Ordination Vows and shirking his responsibilities. Some men defend this attitude on the ground that they can only attend Church Courts at the expense of undone pastoral work — and they are often the very men who, seven days a week are the most conscientious of pastors. Perhaps they need to be reminded that while a Minister ought, for Christ's sake, to be his Congregation's servant, he was never intended to be their slave. Others say that preaching is their main interest and that, in the present state of the Church and the world evangelism is a first priority. Therefore they choose to be evangelists and not ecclesiastics. But this is surely to draw a false distinction. An ecclesiastical historian writing of 19th century Church life in Scotland in the days of the moderates has this to say, "In the 1830's when the evangelicals began to find their strength again, instead of confining themselves to working together for the proclamation of the Gospel they viewed it as their urgent duty to reform the whole Church to which they belonged". Reform, renewal and revival have often gone together in the history of God's people.

Scheming Ecclesiastics

Others see a danger in too great immersion in the affairs of Church Courts and quote Dr. W. F. Marshall's saying that "some men have started out as preachers of the everlasting gospel and degenerated into scheming ecclesiastics". But surely if we remember that the Presbytery and the Assembly are Courts of Christ's Church, if we really believe that of that Church He is the sole King and Head, if we want to see His writ run in every department of the Church's life, then we must not neglect Church Courts, however dull and discouraging they may prove at times to be. To some brethren the General Assembly presents special difficulties because it involves almost a whole week's absence from their pastoral duties. With all respect for their conscientiousness as pastors I venture to suggest that if a week can be given to attend a Conference or a Convention across the water, or to conduct a mission for a brother Minister, then it should not be beyond the bounds of possibility to mark the General Assembly dates in one's diary and to refuse all other engagements but "works of necessity" for that particular week.

Marked Absent

To Elders both Presbytery and Assembly present special difficulties. The businessman does not find it easy to attend

Presbytery meetings during business hours, and businessman and farmer alike find it virtually impossible to give a week to attend at the General Assembly. But then Elders, unlike Ministers, may only be members of the higher Courts very infrequently, due to the rota system operating in their Kirk Sessions. All this makes it difficult for such Elders to take an intelligent interest in the business of the Court or to make worthwhile contributions to debate. It also lends colour to the contention that Church Courts are clerically dominated and that Elders are "lesser breeds without the law". The problem is not easy of solution but one or two things may be said.

More Presbyteries now meet in the evening and this should facilitate the attendance of Elders. Resolutions appended to the Eldership Report presented to last Assembly urged Elders who are not members to attend public Presbytery meetings and also suggested that Presbyteries invite Elders to "sit and deliberate" for a year prior to their actual appointment as Representative Elders. One hesitates to suggest that appointment of Representative Elders should be for a longer term than one year because this would scarcely be fair to the other members of Session, but where it may be possible the idea is worth considering. One other method of improvement is to make full use of the permission granted under paragraph 25 section 2 of the Code for a Kirk Session not sending one of its own members to the General Assembly to nominate an Elder from any other Session in the Church to represent it. Last year's Assembly by resolution urged Kirk Sessions to avail themselves of this facility (Minutes p.54).

Be courteous and not cantankerous

It is sometimes asserted that the present Standing Orders with practically all speeches limited to five minutes make great debate almost impossible and operate unfairly against "opposition" speakers or newcomers to the rostrum. I must admit to a feeling that the interests of debate have been sacrificed to the time schedule, and certainly the flickering light and the buzzer tend to create difficulties for speakers in debate. But then with the increase in Assembly business there is so much to do and so little time in which to do it. All the same, I think present Standing Orders could do with a review in the direction of greater freedom.

Yet, even if a man represents a minority or an unpopular point of view, if he will take the trouble to be informed, if he will try to be courteous and not cantankerous, and can manage to disagree without being disagreeable, then the General Assembly will give him a hearing; and as long as Dr. Weir is at the Clerk's desk he will be sure to get fair play.* Attendance of members at Church Courts and participation by voice and vote when the situation calls for it, is a Christian duty. If we have strong convictions or constructive suggestions let us not fail to raise our voice in their support. Finally, in debate let us never forget that it is always better to divide on a motion that means something than to unite on an amendment that means nothing!

* This was written in 1977 but it is just as applicable to the present Clerk, Dr. Simpson.

MOONEYISMS

No Christian is greater than his prayer life. The secret of praying is praying in secret, but, alas, in the matter of effective praying never have so many before left so much to so few.

In the September, 1985 "Messenger" T.S. wrote, "We are about to begin a new church year... Let each member of Kilfennan therefore determine to make this church year the best ever for — who knows? — it might be our last." And it was his last! He died on January 24, 1986.

Those who love the Lord Jesus never say "Good-Bye" for the last time.

APPENDIX IV

A Study in Contrasts
An exposition of Ephesians Chapter 2

This is one of the mightiest chapters in the New Testament and it can be summarized in two phrases in vv 12 and 13 — "at that time", "but now", and they provide us with a study in contrasts.

Human history has been slashed in two by the coming of Jesus Christ as the calendar recognises, and what was true of human history as a whole was true in experience for the Apostle Paul. There was a time when he didn't know Christ, then there was that great day on the Damascus Road and subsequently years of service to Christ, to Christ's Church, and to Christ's Kingdom. And although our experience may not be so definite, romantic, and devastating as Paul's was, still it is true for all men who are really in Christ, that life for them is divided into two unequal parts as indicated by these two short phrases that summarize the chapter.

It has been said that every heresy that has ever troubled the Church has had its roots in false views of the nature of Man. Paul is prepared to face facts and he takes a dim view of Man without Christ. Indeed he has some devastating things to say about man apart from grace.

First of all, Man apart from Christ is DEAD (v. 1) What are the marks of a dead man? (1) he is incapable of motion, and (2) he is incapable of emotion. He is incapable of action and he is incapable of affection. That is true of the natural man apart from redeeming grace. Therefore it is not preaching the Gospel, even to young people to say 'I challenge you to rise to the height of your manhood and follow Christ.' That's just hot air, and it is no less hot air because it happens to be religious hot air! A dead man can't follow anybody until he gets life, so our first need as sinners is not a challenge to follow Christ but an offer of life in Christ.

It is equally foolish to say to children 'Now boys and girls you must love God' because they can't do it. We can't love anybody to order. Matthew Arnold was perfectly right in saying

We cannot kindle when we will
The fires that in the breast reside.

113

And what is true of our attitude to others is also true of our attitude to God. You can't love God simply because you are told to do it. As someone has said, 'If we force ourselves to perform religious duties we cannot make these duties a pleasure. If we force ourselves to think about God we cannot force ourselves to love Him.' By nature man is dead and cannot follow Christ nor love God to begin with. His spiritual need is so great that the glycerine and rose-water of good advice and good example will never meet his need. That is why preaching as ordained by God is so important in the Christian Church. In Ruskin's words, 'a sermon is thirty minutes in which to raise the dead', though if Ruskin were alive today he would only get twenty minutes or a quarter of an hour! Spiritually, man is dead and needs life in Christ.

According to v.2 without Christ Man is not only dead, he is also DISOBEDIENT. And that disobedience seems to be produced by three things — the influences of the world, the flesh, and the devil.

The world is one of the things that lead people to disobey God's commands. We want to be in the fashion no matter how absurd and daft the fashions may be; but it is very difficult to be 'with it' as far as the world is concerned and loyal to the highest we know as well as obedient to the Will of God.

v. 3 speaks of 'the flesh', which in Scripture is simply 'the self', what man is by nature. Robert Rainy said to his students in Edinburgh, 'Gentlemen, never forget that there is something in human nature that objects to God'.

In modern life this can be seen at work in various ways: in our personal life. You don't generally go to Robert Burns for theology but sometimes Burns said good things and one of them was this,

Thou knowest that Thou hast fashioned me
  With passions wild and strong,
And listening to their witching voice
  Has often led me wrong.

And it works out in our social life. In divorce courts those who once seemed deeply in love now betray their exhausted passions and deflated ecstacy before the gaze of a cynical public.

It is in our political system too. What is meant for the best often becomes the worst; unemployment insurance becomes an encouragement to laziness and the Welfare State becomes a slacker's paradise.

114

And in the world of science you find it also. In spite of great discoveries and achievements the world is trembling on a razor edge between safety and destruction because these terrific powers are in the hands of men whose moral advance has not kept pace with their scientific progress. Personally, socially, politically, and scientifically, the power of the flesh has a bias toward evil and schemes for improvement in all these areas are doomed to fail because they take no account of that bias.

And Paul was old-fashioned enough to think that the devil has something to do with it too (v.2). The intelligentsia might think that the devil is no more but simple folk want to know who is carrying his business on,

> Who dogs the steps of toiling saint,
>   Who lays the net for his feet,
> Who sows his tares in the world's broad fields
>   Where the Saviour sows His wheat?

You have got to reckon with the devil as well as with the world and the flesh.

Even more serious still. Man without God is dead, disobedient, and DOOMED (v.3) The New English Bible puts it like this; "In our natural condition we, like the rest, lay under the dreadful judgement of God." 'The dark line in God's face', as Professor W. M. Clow expressed it, is not a popular doctrine.

A young fellow, who has spent a year at college and had come back knowing everything that was to be known, said to his minister, the Rev. Alexander Frazer (Dr. Carson's beloved old friend and mine) "Mr Frazer, surely you don't believe that a God of love would send me to Hell?". "No, I do not", said Mr Frazer, "but you might get there in spite of Him." This doctrine is part of Scripture and if you take it out of it you will be left with many a blank page in your Bible.

So there is Paul's view of man, not very flattering — dead spiritually, disobedient morally, and doomed eternally. But in a sad doleful world that is not all he has to say. Two great words in vv. 4 and 13, 'But God' throw the shutters aside and let in God's sunlight of good news. Mr. Churchill might ponder what would happen "if God should tire of humanity"; but the Gospel assures us, as Paul well knew, that God will never tire of humanity. The second part of Eph. 2 clearly shows that.

Paul tells us, first of all, that Man is made ALIVE (v.5). The Holy Spirit is the Lord and Giver of Life and in response to

Christ's Cross and man's faith the miracle of New Birth occurs. As the Paraphrase has it,

> 'Tis from the mercy of our God
> That all our hopes begin.

That is where we start — with the Cross of Christ. You see, although man is spiritually dead he is not intellectually dead. He still has got the mind God gave him that is capable of thinking God's thoughts after Him. He is not morally dead for he has got a conscience that tells him the difference between right and wrong. And he is not emotionally dead for he has still got a heart. When the Gospel in all its wonder is presented to man's mind, when it stabs his conscience broad awake, when 'the old, old, story of Jesus and His love' is presented to his heart, then, with his mind to some extent enlightened (which is the first part of Effectual Calling according to the Shorter Catechism), with his conscience convicted of need, and with his heart touched by the story of the love of Christ; then, when in response 'Man commits all that he knows of himself to all that he knows of God', as Billy Graham has put it, then, in His own wonderful way God works the miracle of a New Birth because of the story of the Cross and because of the faith of Man.

The man in the Temple with the withered hand was given the power to do what he was told when Jesus said, 'Stretch forth thine hand' (Luke 3:5). Had he been as logical as us he would have started to argue, but he didn't. He made the effort, and with the effort came the power, and out went the hand. So it is with our faith in Christ. With the Gospel presented to heart and mind and conscience, we are commanded to believe. As Henry Montgomery said to a great audience in the Shankill Road Mission in the old days, 'If I could only get people to trust the Saviour as best they know, how the Saviour would help them to trust Him better'. Trusting Him as best we know, He helps us to trust Him better, and saving faith brings that gift to us and after we have believe we are sealed with the Holy Spirit of promise. Alive!

Such a gift of life will always show itself. Man through the Grace of God is not only alive but also ALERT (v.9). You and I are not saved by good works but unto good works, the good works that follow conversion, that follow our acceptance of Christ, that show the new life that is breathed into us by the Holy Spirit of God. Good works according to the New Testament is not 'do-goodism', not doing a good turn every day. That will make a man a good Boy Scout but it will not necessarily make him a Christian. Good works in the New Testament are done to Christ and out of love for Christ. Four lines that most of us learned as youngsters could not put it better:

I would not work my soul to save, For that my Lord has done;
But I would work like any slave, For love of God's dear Son.

New life shows itself in the activity of good works and also in our love for the fellowship of God's people (v.19). A Christian man, however much he may enjoy the company of those who have no connection with Christ and no love for His Name, specially enjoys, and specially desires, and will always choose, if he has the chance, the company of those who belong to Christ. For a man is not known only by the things he likes but by the things he likes best, not by the things he loves but by the things he prefers when there is a choice to be made.

ALIVE! ALERT! but there is even more to it than that! v.7 speaks of 'the ages to come'. You see, it is not all given here and now. There is still a great future, 'that in the ages to come he might shew the exceeding riches of his grace in his kindness toward us through Christ Jesus'. What does this mean? A negro woman reading that verse was asked that question and she said in reply, 'That means that God is going to point the angels to me and tell them to see what His Grace can do'.

In Rev. 1:5 the redeemed in Heaven are singing a new song, a song with a backward look, a song in praise of Christ that 'loved us, and washed us from our sins in his own blood'. It is a song that even from the glories of Heaven looks back to the sorrows and sins of earth and to the way in which those sorrows are assuaged and those sins forgiven. It looks back to the Cross of Christ and then makes much of the glorious present, 'and hath made us kings and priests unto God and his Father.'

Then the inhabitant shall never say
 That he is sick or sore;
Ne'er complain of desolation
 Or of sorrow on that shore.
And the more this heart of evil
 Troubled him his whole life long,
Now the greater is his gladness
 And the louder is his song.

And all because, as the song tells us, of the blood of Christ.

Is it any wonder that Dr. Alexander Whyte in one of his sermons should say, "Oh, my brethren, what blood the blood of Christ must be! How can even the blood of Christ atone for all my sins? And then not atonement and amends only, not pardon only, but eternal life and all that eternal life is and contains, for the Holy Spirit is the purchase of Christ's blood. A new heart also and a whole new life-time of the means of grace, a peaceful death-bed, a happy resurrection morning, a place at the right hand of the Judge, an open acknowledgement and acquittal on the Day of Judgement and then a mansion with our own name and blood upon its door-post and lintel to all eternity. After the blood has done all this for us, it will abide and will still do the same to our children and our children's children till a great multitude that no man can number have washed their robes and made them white in the blood of the Lamb."

'At that time' . . . dead! disobedient! doomed!
'But now' . . . Alive! alert! awaiting!

And how much we have to wait for. As the countryman said to one of our English poets when asked 'Do you never find life doleful and lonely in this quiet part of the country?' 'Ah no sir, he that aye has something ayont need never be weary.' The Christian aye has something ayont — 'the rapture of the forward view' where

"glory, glory dwelleth In Immanuel's Land."

MOONEYISM

His favourite benediction: *May a dying Saviour's love,*
And a risen Saviour's power,
And an ascended Saviour's prayer,
And a returning Saviour's glory,
Be the comfort and joy of your heart,
AMEN.